Connecting the Fragments

Carolyn Bramhall is living proof that even the deepest issues can be fully resolved in Christ. As a sufferer from DID for many years, she knows what she is talking about. Even better, she has now spent a decade or more living free of it and helping others to take hold of that freedom for themselves. If you want a good understanding of what DID is and how it can be resolved in Christ, it's difficult to imagine a better book to read.

Steve Goss, International Director of Freedom in Christ Ministries

This wonderfully practical volume is a much-needed handbook for those involved in the Christian healing ministry today. It is full of deep insights into the nature of the suffering of those who have been severely traumatised in early life. This book inspires great confidence in the power of Jesus Christ to bring real and lasting healing and liberation through the loving Family of His Church.

Dr Linda Stalley, Co-leader of the Maranatha Community

This is an amazing and practical resource for those wishing to understand and help others overcome extreme trauma and abuse.

Rev. Dr Russ Parker, Founder of Acorn Christian Healing Trust, author and speaker.

This is a remarkable book written by a remarkable person. Within these pages Carolyn shares something of her own experiences and uses them to give us insight into the effects of trauma and abuse. Perhaps what is most notable is that it is all done within the glorious hope of the transformation that Jesus can bring to the darkest of places. Thank you for this book which brings hope and confidence that Jesus, through his Church, can bring healing and restoration to those who have suffered so much.

Rev. John Ryeland, Director of Christian Healing Mission, London.

CONNECTING
THE **FRAGMENTS**

Freedom for people with Dissociative Identity Disorder
in the context of the local church

Carolyn Bramhall

authorHOUSE®

AuthorHouse™ UK Ltd.
1663 Liberty Drive
Bloomington, IN 47403 USA
www.authorhouse.co.uk
Phone: 0800.197.4150

Published by AuthorHouse 01/31/2014

ISBN: 978-1-4918-9019-6 (sc)
ISBN: 978-1-4918-9020-2 (e)

'May the God who gives endurance and encouragement give you a spirit of unity among yourselves as you follow Christ Jesus.'

Romans 15:5

'A small body of determined spirits fired by an unquenchable faith in their mission can alter the course of history.'

Mahatma Gandhi

'Don't walk behind me; I may not lead. Don't walk in front of me; I may not follow. Just walk beside me and be my friend.'

Albert Camus

This book is dedicated to all the saints who have innocently suffered at the hands of others to the point of fragmentation, but who are bravely walking into freedom and wholeness, with their heads high in honour of their King, Jesus Christ.

Names and identifying features have been changed to protect identities, but all the stories are true.

Throughout much of the book we have referred to the survivor as 'she' simply for ease of reading. We acknowledge that all the information relates equally to males.

Contents

Acknowledgements

How can I begin to list those wonderful people who have helped in the writing of this book? The love, friendship and sacrifice that have been the ingredients of my journey to this place are beyond measure, originating as they have from the Source of all self-giving. My life has been richly blessed by those who choose to share their strength and wisdom with me with great generosity.

I will, however, dare to name a few whose support has been invaluable. First of all, my husband, John, whose constancy keeps me grounded, whose quirky sense of humour has us laughing all through the storms, and whose love throughout never wavers. You are irreplaceable; I honour you for sticking by me, and love you for it.

The support from Steve and Zoe Goss and the Freedom in Christ team has been significant and life-enhancing. Thank you a million times. You are truly faith-full and faith-filled saints and I always feel bigger, bolder and blessed when I have been with you.

I must also wave the flag for Joanna McMahon, whose amazing efficiency in—and out of—the office has kept Heart for Truth going when my mind has been elsewhere. Thank you Joanna—you are a true and loyal friend as well as a fun co-worker; whatever would I do without you!

I cannot miss out the rest of the Heart for Truth team. Gerry—your inspirational prayers are woven through the ministry like a golden thread, thank you. Amanda—your friendship has been solid and significant, and means so much to me; Jill—I'm sure you have no idea just how powerful your little notes of love and gifts of flowers, and more, have been in bringing light into the dark times. Bless you for that. To Becky and Martin, Peter, Diana, Mark, Jo

F, Mari and the many others who beaver away in the background to enable Heart for Truth to soldier on while I write, I salute you. Consider yourselves used mightily by our living, loving God.

Lastly, I want to thank all those abuse survivors and those who serve them; your lives have been my inspiration. Some are mentioned in this book, others remain in my mind and heart. I am so grateful to you for allowing me to share a little in your struggles and triumphs. May your faces 'shine with the brightness of his face . . . gradually becoming brighter and more beautiful as God enters our lives and we become like him'. (2 Corinthians 3:17, 18. The Message).

Introduction

Writing a book is such a daunting prospect—especially writing about a subject that is close to your heart. So it is with trepidation that I cautiously attempt to clarify what is, for some, a totally baffling and sometimes scary subject.

I embark on this exploration of Dissociative Identity Disorder partly because I have personally experienced that strange and life-saving condition, so I do know something of how it feels to struggle with the unexplained. Also, because I meet so many people who want to know how to help those who live with DID. Their enthusiasm to understand is refreshing and their love truly inspirational. I write this book with them in mind.

Dissociative Identity Disorder is now becoming more talked about and researched and not before time. For years those who were the victims of horrific abuse or overwhelming trauma were left to suffer in silence. Not now—at least not for the many who are being welcomed into the kind and sacrificial embrace of many branches of the Christian Church. Others, however, are still wandering in a wilderness of misdiagnoses, misunderstanding and harsh judgements. Not every church is helpful; indeed, some are still jumping to the unhappy conclusion that a person acting in uncharacteristic ways must be oppressed, or even possessed, by demons. Such rash judgements have caused untold misery and further trauma.

My prayer is that everyone who reads this may feel moved to reach out in friendship and compassion to those who hurt, whatever their background and social standing, however they behave, and whether or not they are considered to 'deserve' their love. This does not, of course, mean that we are gullible pushovers, easily manipulated into giving people what they demand. On the contrary, with some understanding of the problem, firm boundaries in place and a strong determination to listen to the Holy Spirit as a team, our energies will be effective in leading wounded and troubled people into freedom.

That is the hope and the glory. Sharing in the suffering of others is where our personal journeys touch those 'thin places' where God and man meet in that vulnerable place of weakness and depend absolutely on his mercy. It is there, in the mystery of holy intimacy, that the God of compassion truly shows himself to be our healer.

SECTION 1: FOUNDATION FACTS

Chapter
1

FREEDOM—God's best

'If the Son sets you free, you will be free indeed.'
John 8:36

'I believe that God has planted in every
heart the desire to live in freedom.'
George W. Bush

It is wonderful to belong to the worldwide family of God's
own people. How good it is to have the absolute certainty of
being totally embraced by a heavenly Father. To know you
are loved unconditionally is the best feeling in the world.
However, the journey towards really knowing that awesome
love is a precarious one. Sadly, some don't ever quite make it.

Those who do not understand love
Among those people whose sight of love and security is
blurred, if not completely out of sight, are those who have
been badly hurt early on in their lives, those who have been
abused as infants and small children. Just at a time when
a tiny human is at its most vulnerable, when nurture and
affectionate love is vital, some infants and small children
receive abuse and neglect of the worst kind. Love in any
form is, for them, unfamiliar. So how could they ever
respond to the love of God?

Particularly grim childhood experiences lead an abused
child to develop unique ways of coping. They have to shield
themselves from the full impact of the trauma. Some have

been so severely traumatised that they have had to learn to escape by internally 'going away'. In some cases their minds have consequently split into separate parts (which we call alters, or alternate personalities), and we call this fragmentation dynamic 'dissociation'. Of all people, these are the ones who deserve the most tender and all-encompassing embrace of the Body of Christ. They need this in order to start absorbing the reality that they are loved. For them, dissociation is the way to block off the stunning effects of rejection and cruelty; it allows space for love to creep in. When they meet the love of Christ, demonstrated in his people, there is room for God to begin the work of soothing and healing.

Broken people, broken church

All too often, unfortunately, the opposite is true. More often than not they have been misunderstood and mislabelled, not only by doctors and mental health workers, but also by the fellowships and churches to which they belong. God's command to love all people must not stop at those whose behaviour we struggle to understand. However, it must equally be asserted that those who struggle are not exempt from God's instructions. People who are tormented and troubled will find freedom by following the directions of the Holy Spirit and loving those around them, whether or not they feel understood by them. This is the paradox and the enormous challenge of the Christian life.

Individuals with dissociative disorders may behave in ways that seem bizarre to most of us. But this merely indicates their continuing struggle for survival; they fight overwhelming emotions that surface at unexpected times in disturbing ways. These survivors, who are bravely soldiering on in our churches, are sometimes subjected to long hours of intimidating prayer or disturbing 'deliverance' sessions. Often they seem to bounce from pillar to post; from counselling or prayer ministry to hospital; from psychiatrist to ministry team, in an effort to contain symptoms which make them feel they are going crazy.

My experience of working with troubled people for the last twenty years has taught me that the church in general, and pastoral workers in particular, really do want to see the wounded made whole, often passionately so. However, too often these caring Christians don't know what to do in the face of the mind-blowing disclosures of abuse they hear and the subsequent chaotic lifestyles. Can the church really make a difference to severely traumatised survivors of atrocious abuse? The Bible seems to suggest that nothing is too difficult for the God who created us and that he intends for us all to be whole. Dare we believe that? If we don't, and pick and choose those we welcome and care for, we not only maintain the splitting of one personality, but we keep the church fragmented too. Any local Christian community which fails to love the broken in their midst will itself remain broken.

How to survive
This book is about the way that God has equipped us to not only survive the ravages of trauma in all its forms, but to soar above them. It is about one kind of survival mechanism—the miracle of dissociation mentioned earlier. That is an ability that God has given to some small children who have to cope with the most appalling abuse. It has enabled them to keep going. We are focusing on one 'dissociative disorder' in particular: 'Dissociative Identity Disorder' (DID). It is this way of coping, a way of splitting off parts of our mind to carry the burden of pain, which we will look at in detail.

It is an amazing mechanism and works very well—at least for a small child fighting for survival. However, these children grow into adults who will continue to use this, now redundant, coping mechanism—unless they are led by caring and informed people into freedom, the freedom to be totally themselves, all the time, without fear.

A few years ago a book about dissociation would have been left to collect dust on bookshop shelves. Not any more. DID, formerly named Multiple Personality Disorder, is now a hot topic. Mental health professionals in the UK are thankfully waking up to the plight of those who have not only had to suffer horrific childhood trauma, but also the subsequent misunderstandings, misdiagnoses and mistreatment for the resulting dissociative disorders.

The church's role

Where does the church come in? Jesus Christ has already set us free from the worst of the worst—death and hell. He intends us to live in the freedom of the knowledge that the blow that would have thrown us down into death has now been dealt with—our sin. The life of freedom is God's best for us. He has appointed the church to lead its members into the fullness of joy and knowledge, freedom and purpose.

The Apostle Peter was certain about what we possess as God's redeemed children: 'His divine power has given us everything we need for life and godliness through our knowledge of him who called us by his own glory and goodness. Through these he has given us his very great and precious promises, so that through them you may participate in the divine nature and escape the corruption in the world caused by evil desires' (2 Peter 1:3, 4). We must surely assume here that this applies to all of us, including those who have been cruelly abused or severely traumatised.

God has created humans who are able to create and appreciate beauty, and as such they are unique among all the living creatures on the planet. Perhaps rather than constantly searching for what is wrong or different, and rejecting it, we should be looking for beauty. Neuroscientists are making some groundbreaking discoveries about our brains. For example, it is now known that our bodies hold memories, and that we can help our minds to heal by using our bodies. These discoveries can totally astonish—not because they are entirely new, though they may be to the world of science—but because they are what the writers of the Bible knew all along. We are realising that the scriptures were right in their explanations regarding the way we function. Perhaps God really does know what he is talking about after all.

Beauty, creativity and healing

We really are amazingly like God himself in our ability to create. We are able to recognise loveliness, that splendour which is altogether wonderful, and be awestruck by it. We are able to worship God in 'the beauty of holiness' and sift out the good from the bad. We have God-given abilities to live through pain and suffering and come out the other end free from bitterness and alive with gratitude and hope.

This ability can help hugely in our dealings with broken people. They are beautiful, as Mother Teresa so clearly saw, and their beauty is something that would greatly enhance any church. But first we must understand what has caused the less appealing traits in our troubled friends and seek to help them address these before God. At the same time we must seek to bathe them in the love and welcome of the Good Shepherd who protectively shields his sheep from harm.

We know that in a perfect world, given the right environment, diet and sustenance, many, if not most, of the ailments we suffer heal themselves. Just as our bodies can heal themselves, so can our minds, given helpful conditions and good opportunities for us to choose the right ways to think, feel and act. Alas, we do not live in a perfect world, but we do have a perfect God. So it is to him we look when confronted with the consequences of the evil influences in our lives.

The question must be that either God heals, or he doesn't. If some conditions, brought about by unspeakable atrocities, are just too much for God, then, unimpressed, we must go in search of a bigger 'god'. But if he really does do all that the Bible claims he can, then the issues of severe trauma, indeed, any trauma, however indescribably awful, are ones that he can, in his mercy and power, heal. As we watch him heal just one person, a whole community of God's people becomes a little more whole, a little less fragmented and our faith will blossom enough to see another struggling saint become well. For hasn't God promised that it is the weak that show us how to become strong? 'Listen my dear brothers: Has not God chosen those who are poor in the eyes of the world to be rich in faith and to inherit the kingdom he promised to those who love him?' (James 2:5).

In this book we will work on the assumption that the God of the Bible is who he says he is and does what he has promised he will do. The age of miracles has definitely not passed. I am absolutely convinced that Christian people, ready and willing to 'step out of the boat' and trust him, really will see healing and wholeness come to even the most broken. Our God can indeed connect the fragments of broken lives and broken churches and create beauty amidst the devastation of our fallen world.

Chapter
2

TROUBLES—A tough beginning

'This poor man called and the Lord heard him;
he saved him out of all his troubles.'
Psalm 34:6

'He who knows no hardships will know no hardihood. He
who faces no calamity will need no courage. Mysterious
though it is, the characteristics in human nature which we
love best grow in a soil with a strong mixture of troubles.'
Harry Emerson Fosdick

'The test of the morality of a society is
what it does for its children.'
Dietrich Bonhoeffer

Natalie's story

Natalie turned up at church one morning without realising
quite why she was there. She was woefully thin despite
being heavily pregnant and looked fragile. In time, those
belonging to the church found out that she had suffered
abuse and did their best to support her through the early
years of caring for her baby. It was a struggle: a single Mum
living alone and with little by way of either material or inner
resources.

The church community loved this vulnerable young
woman, who was clearly in deep emotional pain, but as they
got to know her better it became clear that her personality
sometimes took on disturbing and unexplainable changes.

It gradually became apparent that her needs were more complex than they felt equipped to deal with.

Why didn't she get better? They watched with sadness and helplessness as she went in and out of hospital. Her baby was taken into care when she was admitted to the psychiatric ward, her weight dropped to dangerous levels, she self-harmed and talked of, or attempted suicide. She was struggling to look after her own needs, never mind those of her baby.

One of Natalie's friends, Hannah, was stubbornly unwilling to accept that she was beyond help, even though what even the NHS offered seemed to be inadequate. Hannah began to find out all she could about something called Dissociative Identity Disorder as she was convinced that Natalie's extreme and strange reactions lay in that area. Hannah was always there for Natalie as she shared with her the terror of returning memories. She hung in there through the struggles and confusion of not knowing how to react to Natalie's other 'personalities' that appeared when she became too overwhelmed to cope. Over time, Hannah grew to understand her young friend and marvelled at her tenacity and the way she learnt to adapt to life burdened by the stain of horrific past abuse. She was convinced that there was a way through to complete freedom and that that way lay in the hands of the church.

Hannah wrote the following excerpts two years ago, as she spent time with Natalie:

> Natalie's cycle of repeated attempts to function, sabotaged by periods of hospitalisation, went on for some years until the realisation began to dawn that if the church was called to bring in the kingdom of God, if what Jesus did on the cross and in His resurrection really is what his Word claims it to be, then unless we believed that He, and only He, has the answers to desperate situations such as this, we are 'pretending' at being church.

We began to understand that with faith and love we were to bring 'healing to the broken-hearted and set the captives free'. With His leading we saw huge changes as we began to understand the amazing capabilities of the mind to cope in the face of terror, trauma and abuse. We began to grasp how the human mind can fragment in order to survive and then how God can mend; carefully taking those pieces and with loving tender care begin the process of restoration. We saw the power of knowing the truth and the immense inner changes that can bring, even to the most 'hopeless' of cases.

We are still walking out the healing journey with Natalie, but she has an inner stability now which has enabled her to hold down a job, care effectively for her two growing children and loyally supportive husband, and bring order to her inner chaos with the wonderful leading of God's Holy Spirit. She has remained at home and out of hospital for five years now. She hasn't self-harmed for two years, has quit smoking and has maintained a healthy weight for longer. She is bravely facing the harsh realities of her past and the promise of a bright future as the truth of who she is in Christ and what Jesus has done permeates her mind, her heart and her spirit to bring wholeness out of brokenness.

Today, Natalie is totally free and whole, living joyfully and fruitfully as a loving wife and mother. She has even travelled abroad as part of a church ministry team and spoken into the lives of deprived and hurting women in a developing country. That has to demonstrate that this young woman is confident in her new-found self and willing to pour herself out for others.

Jesus can heal all those who come to him. Like Hannah, I believe passionately that nobody is so wounded and damaged that Jesus cannot lead them into a place of freedom. Some, who have experienced abuse so horrific that their minds have fragmented in order to contain and handle those memories, will be sitting in our churches this Sunday.

They will be willing themselves to be 'normal' and doing their best to hold themselves together long enough to keep the rest of the church from finding out just how fragile they really are inside.

The battle for our minds
The challenge for the church is to believe the stories of these broken people, take God at his word and then stay with them until they are whole, embracing them and feeding them with the truth—the teachings of Jesus—because, as Jesus himself said, 'then you will know the truth, and the truth will set you free' (John 8:32).

All hurting people have taken on board a whole package of lies about who they are. That's why they hurt. With the best will in the world, we will not see great results unless the wounded and fragmented know the truth, the deep and integral knowledge they are loved unconditionally, no strings attached, and that they belong to God and that 'the evil one cannot harm him' (1 John 5:18).

As Dr Neil T. Anderson writes and teaches so often, the battle is on for our minds. He has built an entire international ministry, Freedom in Christ Ministries, on the fact that when we really believe who we are in Christ and what he has done for us, astonishing healing and maturity results. So much of our health depends on what we believe, rather then what has actually happened. 'Experience is not what happens to you; it is what you do with what happens to you', writes Aldous Huxley. As we will see later, it is not what happens to a person that causes such far-reaching pain, rather it is the beliefs they have taken away from that experience.

When we are abused as children we will believe the lessons we have learnt from those who hurt us. It is really important that somebody, somewhere, gives us an alternative set of beliefs that teach us we are not useless, filthy or a waste of space, but have immense worth and value. The teaching of these eternal and indestructible truths is not known to be a speciality of the NHS but it *is* something the church can excel in.

My own abuse left me feeling stained and dirty. I wasn't consciously aware of that way of thinking—it was simply an assumption which permeated my every thought and decision for most of my life, even my life as a committed Christian. But one day God got my full attention, the truth dawned, and I walked into freedom—which I possessed all along but just didn't believe.

One survivor of appalling abuse wrote to me recently: 'I remember being led to believe it was my fault and I was responsible for what was happening to me . . . If I did get the courage to tell anyone, who would believe me, who was it safe to tell?' As the mouthpiece of God, we just have to be 'safe to tell' people.

In the coming pages we will take a look at how and why a person's mind fragments into distinct parts in childhood and what it takes for that mind to integrate and become healthy and whole. You will not, however, be offered detailed descriptions of abuse, though we will look at satanic abuse in Chapter 11, nor will we examine the psychological dynamics of the effect of trauma on the mind. There are some excellent sources of information out there which do justice to these important issues. There is a list of helpful books and websites at the back for further reference.

God's people—healing communities

My passion is to see the church, in all its forms, embrace the full truth of God's healing power as he works in and through us as Christian communities. E.M. Bounds wrote in his booklet, *Power Through Prayer*: 'God wants better men not better methods.' Ultimately, it is as we model right ways to think and understand, rather than try to change the behaviours of others, that we will see results. We will become those 'better men' (and women) who are then able to share the 'why' and 'how' of that freedom. We don't need better methods or techniques. In time, the way we act will fall in line with how we think. That precept applies both to us as helpers and to the wounded victim who has yet to learn that they have choices.

I believe that God wants church communities to routinely lead deeply wounded people into an understanding that they really are valuable and cherished. This in turn will bring freedom and joy, so enabling them to become fully functioning, complete and fruitful members of the Body of Christ.

In spite of the burgeoning body of knowledge and information about trauma and abuse, there remains an appalling lack of awareness of dissociation by society at large and even within the medical profession. One woman with DID wrote with exasperation: 'I talk to my GP and she cannot spell "Dissociative Identity Disorder", let alone understand what it means' (Tag e-newsletter, June 2010, www.tag-uk.net).

As both a survivor of Satanic Ritual Abuse and someone who used to have DID, I am now enormously relieved to be able speak about my own past with honesty and without facing widespread unbelief or repulsion. But if my email inbox is anything to go by, many people do not feel or experience such freedom. This email is fairly typical from a husband of a ritual abuse survivor: 'My wife has gone through loads of ministry and deliverance and is under tremendous stress, torment and anxiety. She also dissociates into child and baby alters . . . We have been trying to find help for deeper issues but no one in our area feels equipped or committed to take us through. We are desperate.'

Another husband of a DID sufferer wrote just last week:

> None of the leadership team appeared to understand that hurting people even existed in the church, let alone be able to help and support them . . . I hate to think what damage they are doing to ordinary hurting people . . . I think it is difficult for the average Christian to understand emotional or psychological problems. DID and SRA [Satanic Ritual Abuse] are one step higher than the average problem.

Friends of dissociators are also struggling:

> I have had to gain [the survivor's] trust because Christians who did not know what they were doing have hurt her more. Often they are looking for a demon and forget about the emotional aspects of the person's needs . . . I see great need in the church for people to be healed from so much.

Even more heart-wrenching is the cry of despair from survivors themselves:

> I moved to be near a deliverance ministry, but I got worse. I just don't want to go down that same yucky road again with people who don't understand . . . I don't want to go to someone any more who doesn't know what they're doing. I've been let down too many times.

> I keep asking myself 'am I making this up?' but deep down I know I can't be. Head goes blank. Yes. Blank a lot. It has been blank most of the time these days.

Sometimes survivors have found that they have been misunderstood and even rejected:

> I could never quite 'make it' in life but nobody knew what was wrong with me . . . I had endless times of loving church people misguidedly casting 'demons' out of me . . . the struggle and fight seemed dramatic, so I had no understanding of why the 'clawing' and screaming inside continued.

> Experience has taught me to stay silent. Pastors have ordered me to stay silent. But my silence and isolation don't mean I don't want help.

Although God has equipped us with the ability to heal ourselves mentally as well as physically, we need the right conditions. He has given us a social structure which will provide that healing environment. We call it church. The Body of Christ has been put in place so that God might demonstrate his love and power in and through us, as we love and worship together. This is the challenge and the joy. This is where healing is worked out, lived out and played out. Philip Yancey writes in *What Good is God?*: 'Scientific studies of the effect of prayer on physical healing yield mixed results, but early study verifies that wounded people heal best in a supportive community.' We simply must learn how to be 'safe church'.

I know this to be true from my own rather extreme experiences. I would not be here today if caring Christians both in California and Britain hadn't stepped out of the boat in the middle of the storm. They showed me patience and compassion when my pain was overwhelming both them and me, threatening to throw us all into the heaving, confusing ocean of pain. Although my friends didn't really understand what was going on, they did believe that Jesus could heal all who come to him—even someone as emotionally battered as I was. They persevered by urging me, in every way they knew, to strengthen and reinforce my personal relationship with God—whom to know is real life. This may sound like so much religious patter for some, but I dare to state—no, not just state but loudly declare—that people who have been violated to the point of near insanity are *not* too difficult for God to put together. Furthermore, this happens in the midst of his people, with or without the intervention of mental health professionals.

I firmly believe that healing really can happen for those whose minds have splintered due to the severity of a traumatic past. I believe with passion that they can become whole people. I believe that their healing journey can, and indeed should, take place within the protective and safe arms of their local church community, with the key players being ordinary Christians who dare to believe in the extraordinary power of God's breath in their lives. God can and does connect the fragments of our lives together and form a united body, both in individuals and as churches.

Just before his death, Jesus prayed to the Father for us: 'I have given them the glory that you gave me, that they may be one as we are one: I in them and you in me. May they be brought to complete unity to let the world know that you sent me and have loved them even as you have loved me' (John 17:22, 23).

This uniting does not happen enough, not because churches are filled with uncaring people, but because many Christians just don't know what to do. What is going on, they wonder, when a young woman they thought they knew well, usually so 'together' and so mature, behaves like a frightened child, or an obnoxious teen? How do they protect the rest of the congregation from her bizarre behaviour? And how can they protect her from their stares and sometimes inappropriate, albeit well-meaning, 'ministry'? Why does this have such an impact on the church? What will it take for her to move on into spiritual maturity? Should they refer her to mental health professionals? If so, who are they? Where are they? Could the church's help really be as effective, perhaps even more effective, than professional psychological services?

My hope is that, even though all our questions about DID may not be answered, this humble attempt at reassurance will be inspiration enough to lead these brave and feisty people to a place where healing is eagerly grasped; and that throughout their healing journey the wounded and troubled can remain with the people who know and love them the best—you and I. Remember: 'nothing is impossible with God' (Luke 1:37).

Gaining understanding

'To know that we know what we know, and that we do not know what we do not know, that is true knowledge.' Confucius

There are many things we yet need to learn and it is important to have a teachable spirit. Any way of thinking that closes our minds to further possibilities deprives the thinker of enormous pleasures, surprises and enriching experiences. It is good to be ever learning. As we often don't know what it is we need to learn, we have to keep our minds open and receptive. Sometimes, when we think we have found an answer to a question, we explore the solution so thoroughly we find a hole and fall through into another question. I suppose that is what learning is all about: the journey into ever deeper understanding. Aeschylus, an ancient Greek poet and writer, wrote: 'Learning is ever young, even in old age.'

We must keep our minds open as we explore the wonderful, frightening, alarming and completely awesome ability God has given some to dissociate—to split their mind into parts for the purpose of keeping harmful or disturbing memories and emotions at bay. In learning about this we may find ourselves becoming sceptical, angry, fascinated, appalled or totally disbelieving. That is perfectly in order and allowable. We must face our doubts and ask the awkward questions. Nothing is worth knowing if it cannot stand up to the interrogations of an honest and inquiring mind. I have no wish to 'convert' anyone into my particular way of thinking, but merely to encourage you to consider the facts I present.

Some of those who enter our churches have been so violated that their sense of self has been eroded and they find that they are unable to distinguish between what they choose to do and what others choose for them. They have a weak 'sense of self'. They may find themselves committing acts of atrocity that they do not actually want to do. In fact, survivors may want to deny the abuse ever happened, or that they had a part to play in those acts. The world around them may also want to deny their reality. As if the original trauma isn't enough, the survivor continues to wrestle daily with a world determined to push away the possibility that the great atrocities he/she is struggling to come to terms with were, perhaps are, a reality. Fragmentation is a way of living with that possibility and will be their safety net.

My own childhood was peppered with abusive circumstances. As a troubled Christian adult, my life did not add up. The way I experienced the world didn't match with the way that I perceived others experienced life; neither did my inner, mental processing of the world fit in with the outer, empirical world. I thought there must be a simple explanation for my conflicts. Maybe it was due to a lack of forgiveness towards others or my bad temperedness. Perhaps I was fantasising, making up the voices in my head to attract the attentions of compassionate people in the Christian world in which I lived. Maybe I was looking for praise or to gain brownie points. Perhaps I wanted the attention of those known to minister in certain ways. But no amount of repenting or mending of my ways made life any easier.

It was when, in my early thirties, I was given the diagnosis of 'Multiple Personality Disorder' (now known as DID) that some sense began to emerge and that some order began to appear in what seemed to be a mind in chaos. It also made sense to my husband, who wanted as badly as I did to be able to untangle the sometimes unexplainable behaviour and desperate longings which often drove me to the point of despair.

Emotional trauma has to be treated seriously as it can inflict immense damage, not only on our minds, but also on our bodies. It also has a huge impact on families, friends and communities. We can readily understand that an annoying and unsolved problem can literally give us a headache—a mental issue causes a physical affect. We can also grasp that anxiety can cause our heart to race—an emotional response leads to a bodily one. So in the long term, it adds up that ongoing emotional, mental and spiritual onslaughts can cause injury to our bodies as well as our minds. 'Unresolved emotional pain wreaks havoc on your immune system, cardiac function, hormone levels and other physical functions. We must make peace with our past, because our life may literally depend on it.' (Dr Harold Bloomfield). Even our size can be affected—it appears that the reason I am so short (I am just four feet, nine-and-a-half inches tall) is due to the abuse I suffered at an early age. I failed to thrive.

Imagine the impact on our families and local churches, not to mention the wider communities of which we are a part, if all those who have carried deep trauma were to find healing and peace. The church has got its work cut out, but it is work that is God-ordained and Spirit-enflamed. That means it can be done, and we are the ones to do it.

Dissociative Identity Disorder

So what is DID? Why do I need to understand it? Who has it? Could I have it? Is it catching? Is it curable? Are people who have it dangerous? Would I know if someone had it? How does it begin? How does it end? What is the treatment?

There are lots of questions to be asked, important questions that demand an answer. There are indeed answers to most if not all of them, answers to be examined, pondered on, researched and tested with the most rigorous testing that brilliant minds can subject it to. For DID affects many, many vulnerable people, far more than a few years ago we would have ever dreamt. These are people who have been very hurt, people who are suffering and who deserve to be understood.

Those with a dissociative disorder are really no different from the rest of us. Their symptoms are simply more extreme than most and, of course, the way they have processed and contained their pain may be unique to them, but their basic needs, and responses to those needs, are shared by most of us at some level.

However, in order to effectively address those needs in others we need to come to an understanding of ourselves. In my own life why are there gaps where that sense of being truly loved and accepted should be? Until we get to grips with the thorny issues about what presses our own buttons, until we can fight our own giants, we cannot relate to and understand those with more severe issues at the level they demand or deserve.

As we think about how we can effectively see the most traumatised person come to a place of freedom and wholeness, we need to have a plan of action, some kind of game plan. Goals are always helpful to keep us focused and motivated. When someone has DID that plan becomes something that keeps us from digressing because the presence of alters (or parts), particularly endearing child parts, can hold us up along the way.

Below are some general guidelines that may help as we walk the road to healing with our fragmented friends. This is not a chronological plan, as some items will run concurrently and others will develop in fits and starts, but it may be helpful to have a list to work with. We will address items on the list in more detail as we continue, though we will not use any particular order. The whole recovery journey is undertaken within the embrace of the Body of Christ working within the boundaries of scriptural teaching and Biblical authority.

Ultimately, it is God who heals and he is the one who will be directing our steps. However, some knowledge of the effects of trauma on our minds and behaviours will help us to understand what is happening and why. That does not mean that we will understand everything—it may be that at times we are content to know that as we listen to God and work within the knowledge we have, God will work it for good: 'we know that in all things God works for the good of those who love him' (Romans 8:28).

Recovery plan

1.   Develop a trusting relationship with the wounded person.
Form a team of friends able to offer differing amounts of time and levels of support. Create an environment of safety—a 'Truth Team'. (For more information on Truth Teams contact Heart for Truth www.h4t.org.uk.)

2   Map the inner system.
Get to know the alters.
Help the alters to get to know each other and have relationship with each other. Build an inner team of loving trust and allegiance to Jesus Christ.

3.   Retrieve memories, work with them, reframe them.
Allow amnesic barriers to come down.
Help alters come to terms with what has happened, who they are, why they were created.

4.   Encourage, talk about and experience integration.
Learn new ways of thinking and living.
Plan for the future.

5.   Work on a relationship with God in worship, helping them to understand who they are in Christ.
Be playful and creative and involve friends and team members.
Discover their gifts and ministries.

Chapter
3

TRAUMA—Shaken to the core

'Comfort, comfort my people, says your God.
Speak tenderly to Jerusalem, and proclaim to her that
her hard service has been completed, that her sin has
been paid for . . . the rough ground shall become level,
the rugged places a plain. And the glory
of the Lord will be revealed.'
Isaiah 40:1, 2, 4, 5

'I think the thumbprint on the throat of
many people is childhood trauma that goes
unprocessed and unrecognized.'
Tom Hooper

Let's start by looking at all of us and how we react to the
buffeting that we receive from life.

For decades little tots in Sunday Schools around the
world have sung: 'Jesus loves me, this I know, for the Bible
tells me so.' For those who have been raised within a strong
and committed Christian environment, that love is a given:
we know what it is to be loved. Not so for many of us,
however. Then we have to grapple with what it means to be
loved by Jesus. Do I want that? Can love, whatever that is,
ever lead me to a good place? In fact, can anything lead me
to a safe place? Do 'safe places' even exist, and if they did,
would I ever be good enough or clever enough to find one?

Understanding the laws of love

For many, whose experience of love is confined to shallow, conditional and intermittent affection, the thrill of knowing you're loved is pretty non-existent. Love for them is often linked with sexual performance and punctuated with cruelty or neglect. Worse, for some survivors the abuser also became the Saviour, as it was within their power to bring relief from the pain; to end the torture. Love in that way is, for many, something that has to be endured and the source of love is also the source of pain.

For those who see love in that light, its elusive yet life-transforming power is approached with great caution, if not terror. Something huge and overriding has to happen for them to begin to see love in a new way; to see that it is safe and good; to see that it will take them to a place that previously they could only long for. It will take some time to learn that God really has made a way for them to become all that He intended them to be.

> Fear not for I have redeemed you; I have summoned you by name, you are mine. When you pass through the waters I will be with you; and when you pass through the rivers, they well not sweep over you. When you walk through the fire you will not be burned; the flames will not set you ablaze . . . everyone who is called by my name, whom I created for my glory, whom I formed and made.
> Isaiah 43:1-2, 7

A new start will have to be made; a different set of laws and principles about life will have to be learnt; a whole world view will need altering in order to fully enter into the kingdom life that God has planned. This can be scary for the survivor.

How can this take place? Who will be the teacher? What will it take for him or her to unlearn old ways of thinking, to ditch knee-jerk responses to triggers and learn a completely different, kingdom-of-God way of thinking and being? This total overhaul of a mind does not happen overnight.

It is hard won. It will not happen unless there is a feeling of safety embedded in his/her very bones that gives the courage to start on that journey into what Christians refer to rather glibly as 'healing'. It cannot happen in isolation but occurs within a caring Christian community.

Safe people required

Safe and trustworthy people, who have proved they will not betray or abandon, need to be available. Trust is something that has to grow and blossom as experiences of real love build up over time. Then slowly, oh so slowly, comes that trust that dares to believe that the God of the Bible can and will breathe his peace and cleansing into a hurting and splintered mind.

When we, relatively whole and secure carers and friends of the survivor, trust God, we reflect his beauty and speak his wisdom. But we have to submit ourselves, our whole lives, to his plans in our circumstances. Submission is never easy, that is universally acknowledged. If, however, we have been horribly abused, it is much, much harder and takes a long time to even begin to tolerate the idea of allowing some other power or person any control in our lives. Abuse victims feel that they have had no power of choice at all in their lives; they have grown up thinking that their thoughts, ideas and wishes are of no value whatsoever. They are likely to swing to extremes, either freely allowing others to make all decisions on their behalf (feeling completely incompetent to make good decisions) or they dare not trust anyone. One survivor wrote to me: 'I felt very much a puppet with no thought or will of my own, any slight challenge on my part would lead to more physical abuse . . . The hardest part [of being in a church] was learning to trust somebody. Even now I have a tendency to hide from people, especially Christians.'

But God has a plan and even the most violated, the most burdened, the most wounded of his children are included in it. A.W. Tozer likened God to an architect: he draws up detailed plans for a house. When they are complete he hands them over to the contractor, who gives the work to the brickie, plumber, electrician and so forth. At first the site looks a complete mess, with all the bricks and timbers, earth and machinery lying around the plot. But if you were to come back six months later the building would be complete with a landscaped garden and all looking beautiful.

> We are now to believe that the Father of the everlasting ages, the Lord of all wisdom, has laid out his plan and is working toward a predetermined goal. But all we see is a church all mixed up and sorely distressed . . . and we shrug our shoulders and wonder what is all this, who is behind all this? The answer is that he is the Lord of the ages, he is laying it all out, and what you are seeing now is only the [machinery] working, the truck backed up with bricks; that is all . . . To the uninitiated, everything looks like confusion and turmoil, as though no one is in charge . . . Return in another millennium or so and see what the Lord of all wisdom has done with it. No matter how much of a mess it appears, God has a way of working everything out for his glory.

So many of the hurting people I have had the privilege to meet are longing for this unconditional love with a yearning that is sometimes physically painful. But their entry into our carefully planned-out world comes as something as a shock to our system. It messes up our projects and routines. They are looking for a love that they are not sure even exists, so will take one step forward and two steps backwards. They do indeed appear to be spoiling it for the rest of us. But God knows what he is doing and his perfect plans include them too.

In this lies both the hope and the hopelessness for the survivor. Dare they believe that there is a better way to live, that they can ever be happy? 'How much more disappointed and betrayed would I feel if this turned out to be yet another pipe dream, some cruel trick that God has played on me? Dare I even go there?' We must be careful not to bulldoze through their painful hesitancy and too quickly tidy up the apparent mess they create inside our organised, planned-out world.

The person who is desperate for a love that is stronger than their pain cannot find it anywhere else but in God. However, the uncomfortable truth is that the way for them to understand this love is to find it, first of all, in you and me.

What I am next about to say may cause you to firmly shut this book because many find any treatment of this topic in the context of abuse highly offensive. But I take this risk as I believe it is a key to understanding not just dissociative disorders but the way all of us adapt to life in an imperfect world. From now until the end of the chapter we will look at the basic theology upon which the rest of the book rests.

Talking about the 'S' word

It is all to do with our understanding of sin! 'Sin', wrote Oswald Chambers, 'is not wrongdoing, it is wrong being.' Outside of Christ we are sinners—that is, we live and breathe and think independently of God. When we come to Christ we exchange our old disposition, our old nature, our old being, for a new, God-inspired, God-breathed one. That's what regeneration is. In fact, that's what the cross is all about. Because of Jesus' death, we can exchange our life for his when we commit our lives to him. We actually do, in reality, receive a brand new being, a new life, from God. Then we are 'saved' from old ways of living and the sin that stains us, starting the moment or moments we acknowledged the existence of God in Christ and His momentous act of self-sacrifice for our sakes.

It is not until the seeker grasps this—what actually happened at the moment or moments of becoming what we call a Christian—will they be able to enter the place of freedom and health. Only when they then move on to learn that not only are they no longer a sinner, with a wicked and deceitful heart, but are now a forgiven, clean and chosen saint, will any of our help bring lasting results. They are now redeemed, reclaimed, regenerated. That is the gloriously almost-too-good-to-be-true fact.

I labour this point because you have to know it, believe it and walk in it enough to communicate it—consistently, clearly and effectively—to your wounded friend until they get it, until the penny drops. 'For you were once darkness but now you are light in the Lord' (Ephesians 5:8). Much of what will follow rests upon this.

If freedom is dependent upon what we do or don't do, then the Gospel of freedom in Christ is one of works and is not good news at all. For who of us can maintain good works long enough to really please God? We just can't do that. 'We are by nature, children of wrath' (Ephesians 2:3). If it were true that we have to obey a set of laws then we, in the words of Paul, of all men (and women) are to be pitied (1 Corinthians 15:19). But it isn't like that at all. We are already free because we have been set free by our 'righteousness by faith', our faith in what Jesus has already done for us on the cross. It is not what we do but the realisation of who we are that will enable us to live in freedom—the freedom we already have in Christ. This is all the good news, the Gospel of truth.

Forgiveness and fruit

Let's take a very hard-nosed look at the wounded people we know. If we read the list of sins in Galatians 5:19-21 we will see traits we recognise in them (and in ourselves). At least some on this list are almost everyday occurrences: discord, jealousy, fits of rage, selfish ambition . . . envy. We must try to put aside for a moment the knowledge that these reactions are very understandable, given the trauma or pain or difficulties that our wounded person has had to endure and, therefore, are perhaps excusable. In no way can we suggest that inflicted pain upon a child was the child's fault, or that it was her wrongdoing that caused such unspeakable horror. It is *never* a child's fault. But we can step out boldly here and say that all of us, including those who have been ill-treated, are in need of forgiveness.

Jesus never did make excuses for people. He delivered the Sermon on the Mount—which includes some very uncompromising and quite demanding instructions—to the very poorest of the ordinary people in the locality. Remember they all herded out to the hillside of Galilee to hear Jesus speak. The crowd included the very young and the very old, the poor as well as the rich. Most would have had little or no schooling apart from a few years of instruction that boys were given by the local rabbis. There would also have been many sick people among them—no NHS there, or even trained medics as we know them. So those who were physically sick, mentally unwell and materially poor would have been listening to Jesus that day. They were the 'little people': insignificant, lowly, working people, from the country districts of ancient Palestine.

Jesus made no compromises for them, or for any others we read about in the Gospels. He didn't, for example, run after the rich young ruler when he rejected Jesus' command to turn his back on his material wealth. Jesus did not give him some other, easier route to the 'eternal life' he was seeking. (Mark 10: 17-23). He didn't call out, 'No, OK, maybe giving away everything is too much to ask. What about if you started to give away just a bit? Let's take it slowly.' There is no evidence that Jesus wanted to bend the rules for anybody in order to make it easier to enter his kingdom. We have to arrive at the stark realisation that if we try to be as perfect and sinless in our own merit as God needs us to be in order for us to know him, it 'just ain't gonna happen'. We can therefore safely assume that even the most fragile survivor will need to come to a place of repentance before a saving, gracious Father God in order to begin to find relief from the fears and shame with which they are burdened.

Next take a look at the list of the Holy Spirit's fruit in Galatians 5: 22-23: Love, joy, peace, patience, kindness, goodness, faithfulness, gentleness, self-control. Are they not traits we want for the wounded people in our lives? (Those are the qualities I long for in my life too.) But those are fruit and fruit grows as a natural turn of events—the watering and feeding of a healthy plant. An apple tree does not try hard to produce apples. Given the right soil and conditions, it just does, because that is what it is made for. Given the right conditions, we will produce those fruit in our lives, for that is what we were made for. So we can, indeed, expect good and positive feelings and attitudes to emerge from our survivor friend as they are daily filled with God's Spirit of grace.

When the wounded person finds real forgiveness from the sin and the 'stuff', the chaos and the crimes of the past, he or she begins to breathe the pure air of freedom, with or without psychological help. What we want them to know is that there is infinitely more goodness and glory in living than they could ever have imagined. Life is so often a heavy weight that some survivors would like to end it. One survivor, 'Katy' wrote: 'I guess death was the ultimate, and very often I would wish they would kill me . . . I did attempt suicide many times but God had other plans for my life.' Many, like Katy, cannot see any hope of a life of fun and freedom.

C.S. Lewis wrote in his sermon, *The Weight of Glory*, something quite telling that finds a joyful resonance in many:

> We are half-hearted creatures, fooling about with drink and sex and ambition when infinite joy is offered us, like an ignorant child who wants to go on making mud pies in a slum because he cannot imagine what is meant by the offer of a holiday at the sea. We are far too easily pleased. There is so much more for us, who are easily satisfied with mud-pie lives for ourselves and those we care about.

Understanding people—can we?

There are two things we need grasp about people. The first is that we are all different. The second is that we are all the same.

There is no way I can claim to fully understand you and there is certainly nobody who really understands me (ask any husband). There is a fridge magnet that says, 'Don't try to understand me, just love me.' Even people who have been brought up in the same house by the same parents, dressed in the same clothes, had the same holidays and eaten the same food, will be different in the way they see things. We each have a slightly different angle on the world—what you see and hear, even at the same event, will be slightly different from what I see and hear. It is, indeed, important that we are not the same. Someone once said, 'If two of us were identical, one of us would be unnecessary.' So I dare not say that I really 'know' what it is like to be you. Even though I may be able to identify with some of the things you are going through, I will not know exactly what it is like to walk in your shoes.

On the other hand, we are all the same. We all have longings, desires, needs and aspirations and even though they may seem to be diverse, they all boil down to three baseline needs that all humans have. They are the need for security, the need for significance and the need for acceptance (I am indebted to the teaching of Dr Neil T. Anderson for these three concepts).

Security, significance and acceptance
We all need **security**. We need to feel that our needs are going to be met, that we will have a roof over our heads, food in our stomachs, provision for the future, people around us, health today and help when our health fails tomorrow. For some, the need for security is their life's driving force; it's what keeps them doing what they do, and going where they go.

If we don't feel secure we will find someone or something that gives us security, or at least the feeling of security. Some teach a small child to find security by giving it a dummy (comforter). What they want is Mummy's warmth and presence, but failing that, something that reminds them of that comfort. Something that resembles a nipple, say, will have to do. The dummy, or a thumb, will have to work as a substitute for the real thing. Later in life, putting something in their mouth is a natural response to give them the feeling of security, as though their needs are being met just by having oral comfort. It is a deception of course. So eating, smoking, drinking, drugs, even chewing gum, will all appear to go some way to meeting that need. The trouble is it doesn't last. In fact, when the cigarette is finished, when those chocolate biscuits have gone, the temporary satisfaction is replaced by a sensation of being let down, and the low is lower than before. So we have to find ever more extreme forms of satisfying that need, or find ways to blot out that need altogether, or even create a bigger need to distract us from the disappointment of the first.

We also have a very basic need for **significance**. People need to feel that they are important; that they have a role, a place, that they belong and fill a slot in the world that nobody else can fill. Our need for significance can take us to great heights as we seek to be the first in this or the best in that. It is this need that propels much of the world of media. Television programmes in which contestants compete for recognition of their performing talents—*Britain's Got Talent*, *The X Factor* or *Strictly Come Dancing* at the time of writing— are highly popular. They wouldn't be such a success, in fact they wouldn't exist at all, if it wasn't so very important to us to been seen as particularly gifted in some area. To be praised and exalted for what they can achieve is the be-all-and-end-all for many in the present generation.

Without significance I am a Nobody. Perhaps I was told as a child that I would never amount to anything, that I was a nuisance. Or maybe I felt tossed around: lots of house moves, changes of friends, schools, families or locations will contribute to a feeling of insignificance. Not finding your place or your niche is an uncomfortable feeling. 'I am in the way, and who I am is of no value. I don't really fit anywhere; you can live very well without me' is what so many feel.

Today in Britain, indeed in the West, it seems that the biggest, the loudest, the most talented and most accomplished win all the acclaim and recognition. We long for recognition, so if I am not accomplished or gifted I will be relegated to second – or last – place. It is important that other people see me as of value because without your reassurance I cannot believe that I am important at all. If I am not special then why am I here? What good am I? Many of those unfortunate enough to be unemployed suffer acutely from feeling that they are insignificant. If my job determines who I am, take my job away and what am I left with? 'I don't know who I am any more. Perhaps I am, after all, just a Nobody.' That is excruciating.

The other basic need we have is to be **accepted**. As a counsellor I doubt that I have ever seen anyone about anything for whom rejection is not a major part of their problems. To be abandoned, rejected, ignored, neglected, disliked or hated is so very, very painful. It is the ultimate offence, and one in which Jesus shares so intimately with us. 'He was despised and rejected by men, a man of sorrows and familiar with suffering' (Isaiah 53:3). God's unquestioning acceptance of all, regardless of status, background, creed or performance, is the most powerful colour on the canvas of the church's work of art which displays Christ in the world. I want to be wanted. I need to be needed. 'Will somebody please love me, like me, choose me.'

We have an insatiable need to be accepted. Love is based on unconditional acceptance. Will you embrace me for who I am, with all my faults and foibles, with all my traits and talents? Will you choose to receive me as I am? When I do not feel accepted I may try extremely hard to play a part, adopt a persona that I think will be more acceptable to you. If I act in this way you are bound to accept me, because then I will be like others whom you accept. The Jesuit John Powell wrote a book entitled, *Why Am I Afraid To Tell You Who I Am?* In it he tells of a real conversation in which somebody's answer to that question was: 'I am afraid to tell you who I am, because, if I tell you who I am, you may not like who I am, and it's all that I have'. How scary to feel that if you really knew me, then you would go away. We would live our lives trying hard not to be ourselves, believing that our 'self' is just not good enough.

I may withdraw and try not to be seen at all so that I do not have to be reminded that you may not like me. Powell writes, 'To reveal myself openly and honestly takes the rawest kind of courage' and yet, to live without self-disclosure cuts us off from real encounters with others and is such an unfulfilling way to live.

On my first visit to California I was invited to a Christian women's meeting held in someone's home. The house was full when my friend and I arrived. All the women there seemed so confident, open and joyful. Most knew each other well. On entering I had to walk into a room full of noisy, happy women, all of whom looked at me with interest, regarding me as a cute little English woman, the newcomer, the stranger. I wore different, darker clothes, did not wear bright lipstick or long earrings and felt dowdy and boring.

I absolutely hated it. I sat in a corner and hoped fervently that they would forget about me. I did not feel in any way like them. I could not imitate their confident speech or their joke-telling or loud laughter. I just wanted to get out. I *assumed* that because I was not like them that they would not like me or be able to accept me. If only I knew then, what I have since discovered, that the reverse was true. I was just not aware that simply by being myself I was accepted and had a place in their gathering. They admired my English accent, my British education, my experience of the world that was so different from theirs. Instead of enjoying their genuine interest I shrank in the corner and dared not open my mouth.

The pain we suffer when we don't feel that we have one or all of these three—security, acceptance or significance—can be acute and unbearable. Therefore, we will often go to great lengths to find them. God knows that we need them, because he made us and only he can truly meet those needs. The reason we will spend most of our lives looking for them is because we choose to try and meet these needs ourselves, needs that only God can fulfil. So *of course* we will feel dissatisfied.

We only really feel secure when we know that God has met all our needs in Jesus Christ. We only really feel significant when we know deep inside our psyche that we are chosen by God to be his co-worker. We only really feel accepted when we know that we are loved unconditionally by a God who has no favourites, who loves us for who we are, not what we do. That his love is based on his nature not on ours. '"The Lord did not set his affection on you and choose you because you were more numerous than other peoples," he said to the Israelites, "*But it was because the Lord loved you* . . . he is the faithful God"' (Deuteronomy 7:7-9, italics mine).

We must realise that the pain that triggers dysfunctional lifestyles is driven by the search for security, significance and acceptance. At the back of all the symptoms of the mental and emotional aberrations we come across, including dissociative disorders—especially dissociative disorders— is a deep-seated grief for the loss of 'something' without which we cannot survive. These largely unrecognised and unspoken feelings are so strong they will drive a person to the most extreme lengths, and sometimes right over the edge and into psychosis or death. The pain of feeling that the only value I have is as the focus of sexual attention or an object which satisfies the base and repugnant desires of others, is acute.

Needs and longings

That is why I say that we are all the same, for we all have that urgent drive in some measure to fill those needs. For those of us with fairly comfortable lives, we can hide those needs with false comforts that disguise the pain of living without the God who meets our deepest needs. The Bible is full of reminders that God is the only one who can really fulfil all our longings: 'He satisfies the thirsty and fills the hungry with good things' (Psalm 107:9). When Jesus came and died for us, mankind was at last able to enter fully into that most satisfying of relationships: 'Whoever drinks the water I give him will never thirst. Indeed, the water I give him will become in him a spring of water welling up to eternal life' (John 4:14). We all must come to that place of recognising our need of God, and then turning round to face him. As author and evangelist J. John puts it, 'There are two sorts of people in the world—those who are prodigals, and those who were' (*The Return: Grace and the Prodigal*).

If we don't believe that Jesus can ultimately satisfy not only my need in every way but also in all who come to him, including and especially those who are deeply wounded, then we will spend much of our time seeking out answers elsewhere. It can be an exhausting and all-consuming pursuit.

I had spent three and a half years living alone in California, with my husband and children six thousand miles away. I then spent another seven years in England completely submersed in my inner pain, digging through the most wretched memories of abuse and cruelty. Not surprisingly, I despaired of ever finding peace. It felt as though my mind was so overwhelmed with horrific memories and tortuous feelings that there would never be a time when there could be room for good ones. The search for that all-too-elusive answer seemed to be taking over my life to the exclusion of everything else. I had concluded that it was all down to not having enough money. If only I could afford to get to that healing centre or see this therapist or attend that conference, then everything would be alright. If only I was able to have the right person pray for me and belong to the right kind of church, healing would come.

I was wrong to believe that, and thankfully I met some people who taught me one of the most amazing and mind-blowing lessons of my life: freedom was within my grasp— and had been all along—because freedom is found in knowing, really knowing, who we are in Christ.

With their coaching I began to really believe what God said about who I was, who he is and what he has done for me in Christ—I mean *really* believe it, with all my mind, with everything that I could summon up from deep within. This gradually awakened a sense of giddy joy. I am free in Christ! Coming to that wonderful realisation completely changed my life.

I am not saying that this is easy—not at all. It took me months of working hard at really 'getting' the truth (and I am still working on it). I already had some grasp of the Bible due to Bible College training and understood a great deal about dissociation and how it worked in my life. But what I knew as theory and what I intrinsically believed in my bones, in the very fabric of how I functioned, was something else. I worked very, very hard in those first few months. It was painful and seemed to go against all I felt. But the effort was worth it and the impact on my life was huge—for a start I didn't need the old coping mechanism of switching into other parts, or alters. Everything changed.

I turned right around. The past really was, for the first time in my life, the past. I could get up in the morning and look forward to a new day unsoiled by bad memories, untainted by the dread of what may happen because I had spoken out the unspeakable about my past. My life started to become sunny because my heavenly Father spoke into my heart that I was a delight to Him. He was proud of me. I was thrilled! A relationship with God began which was based upon love instead of fear, and it changed the way I saw myself, my family, my life, the world—everything.

Before we launch into a helping role within our churches, God wants us to line up our way of seeing people with his own. How we see others is vital to the way they react to us. Conversely how another sees you depends on how you see him. So when we see that 'poor soul' who has suffered so much and now acts in ways that we can't fathom—the one whom we tend to avoid—we can now see them as someone who is simply desperate to find security, significance and acceptance. Just like you and me, in fact. They are motivated by that which also drives us. As we find the way to being fulfilled in God, so we can point the way for our struggling survivor friends to follow. And as the wounded recognise that we can identify with them, they will gradually begin to trust us.

Fellow travellers

What has this to do with equipping the church to help people with DID? We simply have to stop seeing these deeply wounded people as in a different category or from a different stock of people to ourselves. They are fellow travellers. There is a saying, 'We get to heaven together or not at all.' The Christian life is all about togetherness, the ability to see Jesus in each other, indeed, to *be* Jesus *to* one another. Philip Yancey, in his book, *What Good is God?* writes this: 'I have a hunch that if the watching world saw the church as a place that welcomes broken people for healing, it might have a greater impact than all our sophisticated outreach programmes put together.' It is in our relationships that God is most able to bring healing and the long-term support and security that allows it to be sustained.

SECTION 2: PIPPA'S PROGRESS

Chapter
4

COPING—Ways and means

'Be strong and courageous, and do the work. Do not
be afraid or discouraged, for the Lord God, my God,
is with you. He will not fail you or forsake you.'
1 Chronicles 28:20

'Someone who has experienced trauma also
has gifts to offer all of us—in their depth, their
knowledge of our universal vulnerability, and their
experience of the power of compassion.'
Sharon Salzberg

Some people know all about dissociation. For instance, a
husband has been known to pick up a newspaper at the
end of the day and be utterly absent as far as his wife is
concerned. He hears nothing. Children are good at this
too. I had the pleasure of spending a morning with a five-
year-old boy a while ago. I had dug out my old biscuit
tin of plastic animals, toys out of Christmas crackers and
other little figures that had accumulated over my years of
motherhood. He soon became completely engrossed in the
story of the zoo he had created, with a farmer in charge of
all the little creatures (and things that passed as creatures).
Little Adam was totally absorbed in the unfolding tale of his
zoo and the adventures and conversations of the animals.
That world became his reality until it was time for him to go
home. That little boy had, in some sense at least, *dissociated*

from the reality of my kitchen table and was totally absorbed in the scenario he had created.

Highway hypnosis and other marvels

While returning home in your car, have you ever arrived having driven along busy roads and negotiated turnings and traffic lights, but without apparently having thought about your driving at all? Long distance travelling is even easier to 'forget'—your mind can be somewhere else, while you jet along the motorway, controlling (hopefully) your speed and making dozens of snap decisions that keep you and other road users safe. That dynamic is known as 'highway hypnosis'.

What is happening here? Neuroscientists have discovered what mothers have known all along, that we can do more than one thing at a time. We speak of being 'in two minds' when trying to make a decision, or refer to someone who is very anxious as being 'beside themselves' or 'out of their mind with worry'. We even speak of being 'shattered' at a piece of bad news, as if our minds have been broken into fragments by the shock. We instinctively know that we have dialogues going on in our heads, particularly when having to make choices. The process of 'choosing' is a very complex one and involves looking at facts, acknowledging feelings and arriving at conclusions. We are caught up in it many times a day. We do indeed seem to have more than one mind and 'I, myself and me' do not always agree.

It is that ability to shuffle facts and feelings around in our minds that can actually keep us sane and alive. Our brains are always seeking organisation and clarification to fit our experiences into what we know of our world. So we process the information in order to make sense of it and to know where to put it in our thinking. We do this processing in different ways and dissociation is one of those ways. When external circumstances are so dire, feelings so intense or pain so acute that we are overwhelmed, we are actually able to make the decision to block out much of the adverse experience. In fact, when small children, who most easily dissociate, do the blocking, it can become a life-saving coping mechanism. In adulthood, too, we are sometimes able to 'turn off' some unpleasant or painful present experience, and push it into a deep, dark corner of our minds. This tends to happen in events such as a violent encounter; in sexual, physical or emotional abuse or after a bad traffic accident or some other traumatic experience, as in war atrocities. Sometimes that pushing-away dynamic is so effective that we may have subconsciously chosen to forget it altogether in order to avoid the pain that recalling it would evoke.

Post-Traumatic Stress Disorder

This repression can later return to haunt us and intrude in such a way that it can dominate our lives. That's what happens in Post-Traumatic Stress Disorder (PTSD). The memory of a traumatic event gets relegated to a part of our brain that holds it until things settle down for us. When we are in a place of relative safety, the memory may begin to resurface, having been triggered by a sound, sight or smell reminiscent of the original trauma. The memory seldom returns all at once, but 'flashes' of it might appear in the consciousness at random times. The sharp crack of recall, the sudden image of the sounds of tyres skidding or the breaking of the windscreen, the smell of the casualty department—such 'flashbacks' may suddenly come and then leave just as quickly, leaving the victim experiencing the same terror as on the original event. The brain is busy trying to process the event, but it can take hours, days, months or longer to recover from the flashback, leaving with it the dread of it returning.

Post-Traumatic Stress Disorder (PTSD), as unpleasant as it is, has its purpose. It has enabled the victim to return to some kind of normalcy immediately following the traumatic event, giving their system a chance to heal before it gradually re-introduces the memory, bit by bit, back into consciousness. Sensitive and caring support and the space to talk about and reframe the shocking events really help recovery. With the sure knowledge that God was, and is, ever present, healing can and does occur. The splitting off of one part of the consciousness from another has played its God-given role. Healing is particularly complete when the Holy Spirit is allowed to breathe into our minds the deep peace of God.

The purpose of dissociation

But what happens if the traumatic events are many and random? What happens if the trauma is an integral part of life? Can an individual push large tracts of traumatised memory away? The answer is, yes. God has provided us with the equipment, in certain situations and with certain people, to dissociate; in this case, we split off whole blocks of time. When the trauma is over we are then able to pick up the threads of the untraumatised part of our lives and our personalities and carry on where we left off. This ability is most effective in small children, before the age of around six or seven, when their personality is still flexible and able to be easily moulded. It is alarmingly easy to shape a young life and shocking items on the news attest to widespread use of that ability to manipulate the minds of little ones.

Small children are constantly absorbing the attitudes, atmosphere and messages around them. They learn hundreds of new things every day, forming a picture in their minds of what life is all about. They learn who they are, what is expected of them, what feels good and what doesn't, what brings rewards and what brings punishment, and how to get attention and affection. So many new facts bombard their minds in their early years. Most of what we learn in terms of who we are and how safe the world is for us we find out before we even start school.

Being so pliable enables parents and significant others to introduce to their young charges the principles that are important to them. As Christians we take very seriously the moulding of young minds and aim to build very carefully and sensitively on the inherent ability of small children to recognise and know a loving and kind God.

Unfortunately, this pliability can be and is used for evil purposes. Satanists, paedophiles and others strive to gain access to small children in order to groom them for a lifetime of usefulness to their purpose and they are frighteningly successful. Often, by the time a child reaches puberty he or she can be completely brainwashed into believing the values of those who have influenced them. We can only make healthy choices if we have been given the options and understand the consequences. If a child is only told the negative consequences of not obeying the (possibly evil or harmful) rules of a family group or cult, their choices only have to do with survival: 'If I do what they want me to I might not get hurt again.' That is all that matters. Every child has a right to be given a full range of options for their lives, including and especially the truth of the Gospel of Jesus Christ.

Where does dissociation come in all of this? Where a child is subjected to abuse as a way of life, survival choices have to be made. Dissociating, or splitting off, the painful reality of the present is a sensible choice for an abused child.

Meet 'Pippa'

For the purposes of this book, let's imagine a scenario. We will follow the journey of trauma and recovery of a fictional little girl. We'll call her Pippa. As a small child she is told that she is pretty and is a good girl. She is given sweets and treats; has birthday parties and summer holidays; even has cuddles (but these are not given consistently, so could not be counted on). What she doesn't know is the agenda of the adults in her life. Nor does she understand the randomness of the good times. She will, as all small children do, see her parents as all-knowing and all-powerful. She has to— it would be intolerable for her to think otherwise, given that she depends completely and utterly upon them for her survival.

Then comes the really confusing part. Sometimes bad things happen to her. They are frightening and make her feel lonely. She is visited when she is in bed at night.

Sometimes she is taken to other places and shocking things take place both around her and involving her. Little Pippa becomes uncertain about who she is, who she can trust, who is good and who is bad. She is told that this is necessary for her and yet it feels wrong, yucky. She can never fully prepare herself for the unpleasant times because she can never really be sure when they will happen. Therefore, in order for her to be prepared, she learns to be constantly vigilant, anxious and hyper-aware.

The most difficult thing is how to fit in her painful, sometimes terrifying experiences of abuse with what she has been taught and believes to be true: that her parents and those she relies on to meet her needs are good and can be trusted. 'They can't be wrong or bad. It must be me that's bad. It must be my fault that these horrible things are happening.'

There are ways of handling unpleasant experiences: some people shut down, others become 'invisible', while others may black it out. But for some the best way of effectively coping with this hugely perplexing and chaotic jumble of conflicting beliefs and experiences is to dissociate. 'This is too painful to bear, so I will go away and find someone else inside me to come and take my place. I will call him Jimmy. He is a naughty boy and deserves to have these bad things happen to him.' When the abuse ends, 'Jimmy' can go away and it is safe for Pippa to return, happily with no knowledge or memory of what had transpired while Jimmy was in the body. The ability to dissociate, to partition off, has allowed Pippa to resume her life in some semblance of normality.

But Jimmy, having been brought out on a number of occasions, forms a memory bank of his own. He is 'out' so often that he has the beginnings of a personality and character. But supposing he gets pushed to the limits of his endurance? If Jimmy was created by Pippa to handle sexual abuse by, say, an uncle, when she is exposed to a whole group of people who want to use her, he is not equipped to handle the extremes of terror and confusion that that initiates. So then the same dissociative dynamics take over and someone else 'appears'. Let's say Pippa then creates a part she calls 'Molly'. Jimmy and Pippa retreat deep inside the psyche and Molly stares wide-eyed, not knowing where or who she is and accepts the treatment.

Remember that this is all happening in a very small child whose reality has not been already shaped and moulded by years of experience in the real world. This is reality for her; this is what she will believe is the normal way to live. It will be years before she will have the opportunity and understanding to objectively look at her experience of childhood and compare it to that of her healthy, adequately cared-for friends. It is only then that the realisation dawns that she has been cruelly exploited, and the 'hell' begins.

So Pippa has Jimmy and Molly to call upon when circumstances demand it. For some, the abuse becomes ever more cruel or bizarre. So, like Pippa, they may have to create other 'parts' to deal with, say, physical abuse like scalding, beatings or deprivation of food or water. Some children have to endure psychological abuse, such as being forced to watch the cruel killing of a much loved pet, or (as is sometimes the case in Satanic Ritual Abuse) given the choice between being abused herself or having a sibling or friend take it in her place. Sometimes the unthinkable happens and Pippa has had to watch or even take part in appalling rituals. The shock to her fragile developing sense of self will be felt for the rest of her life. (The subject of Satanic Ritual Abuse will be explored further in Chapter 11.)

You will have got the message now: God has lovingly equipped small children to psychologically escape, albeit temporarily, from the full force of the painful and totally untrue messages the abuse gives her. She thinks: 'I am bad and deserve to be punished. In fact I am so bad that I deserve to be punished in really tortuous and unspeakable ways. My only worth is in how useful I can be to others.' Other lies will grow from those initial beliefs: 'I am different from other people'; 'If I don't look after myself, nobody else will'; 'No one is trustworthy'; 'I am dirty and can never be clean'; 'Good things will never happen to me' and so on.

Pippa may later, in adult life, discover that she has completely repressed and hidden whole swathes of her childhood experience. However, people like her also often struggle with deep-seated fears and misconceptions. These have grown as part of the survival 'clothing'—'if I don't trust anybody then I am less likely to be betrayed and abused. If I don't expect anything good then I won't be disappointed.'

So God has provided ways of escape—amazing ways that ensure the sanity and survival of the weakest and most vulnerable. This is the miracle of dissociation.

Dissociative disorders

Dissociative *disorders* are an entire group of mental conditions in which a person, usually a survivor of extreme childhood trauma, routinely dissociates. In various stages of severity, they split off part of their mental functioning and part of their consciousness changes, so affecting their functions of identity, their memory retrieval, their thoughts, feelings and experiences.

Pippa, therefore, is only functioning with part of her full personality at any one time. She is not able to completely enjoy who she is as a unique and precious person, made in the image of God and valuable to him.

The dynamics of dissociation

During the time when a person is dissociating, certain information will not be processed in the normal way—it will be siphoned off into another part of the consciousness and the normal connections with other information will not be made. This provides a temporary escape from the reality of painful and traumatising events. But this may affect their sense of history and identity.

We are seeing an increasing number of survivors emerge in the church, with just such an ability to dissociate and showing evidence of other 'parts' or 'alters'—alternate personalities. Why are they suddenly coming forward? We are speaking about abuse and its aftermath much more openly in society at large and inside the church. But there is still a way to go before survivors will feel completely at ease in our fellowships.

When they are with others, what triggers them into actually 'switching' into that other personality? What makes an adult with a history of dissociation leave the here-and-now and retreat into the depths of her being, allowing alters to take executive control of her actions and words? What is it that triggers that process in an adult who left the actual danger behind long ago?

There is a logical process which leads someone with an already established dissociative propensity—and who has developed a dissociative disorder—to having a full dissociative episode. Their goal is to back out of the here-and-now and push another part of their consciousness forward to take charge of the situation. There are various factors that contribute to this situation:

1. General triggers

What is it that would make the adult Pippa retreat and give space for Jimmy or Molly to take her place? First of all there are the non-specific triggers which are the general background stresses in her life, such as relationship difficulties and work pressures. If Pippa's workplace was undergoing some changes or if the weather was cold and bleak she may feel more vulnerable. Any one of us would have to step up our coping strategies slightly to handle these things, though most of us wouldn't be conscious of anything more than mild irritation. It is more difficult for those with a dissociative disorder.

2. Personal factors

In addition, some extra stress-producing situations may be occurring. These could include ill-health, hormone imbalance (time of the month, pregnancy, menopause, etc.), medication adjustments and other personal changes. In that case Pippa's stress levels would go up a little more.

3. Current life events

Current life events could exacerbate the situation further. Any sign of additional emotional demands which may result in anxiety and depression like bereavement, internal conflict, sleep disturbance, or perhaps issues emerging in therapy or in her chats with the church pastoral worker, would increase her susceptibility. At this point, the adult Pippa would struggle to maintain balance.

4. Issues closer to home

The last straw would be that tricky situation: harsh or unfair words, certain triggering phrases, images, sounds or smells that reminds parts of her mind that this situation is not safe. In her weakened and more fragile place it would not take much to tip Pippa into switching into an altered state of consciousness. Then she would dissociate from the here-and-now, just as she did when she was being abused as a small child. She knows how to escape from unpleasant things and does is without being aware of it.

These were experiences I lived with daily for years, so here I will try to describe what it was like for me when I felt pulled into dissociating. I suspect things are not so different for many others.

First of all I would be vaguely aware that I was coming to the edge of my ability to cope—in fact I may have felt like that for days (there would probably be good reason). The palpitations would start; my heart would bang and the 'uh oh' would resonate inside. Then, at the tipping point, the strangest thing would happen: it would seem as if everything around me was fading into the distance. Even though I could still see and hear perfectly well, it would all seem as if life was happening an increasingly long way off, or as if it was taking place in a dream and didn't really involve me.

My vision would seem to narrow, like having blinkers at the side of my eyes, a kind of tunnel vision. My hearing would seem less acute, woolly and I would be in a dreamy bubble that separated me from the rest of the world. The bubble would protect me. I was safer there and didn't want it to burst. That bubble was a good place to be and I just didn't care what happened next. I would not so much lose control of my body and mind as much as happily hand over control to someone else. That someone else was actually still me, but only a shadow of who I was as the in-control adult.

Sometimes I was perfectly aware of what was happening in the real world. I could hear the words coming from my own mouth, see the people around me and yet I was not touched by it all and didn't want to intervene. I would think, 'this isn't my concern; it is not my responsibility.' I not only couldn't intervene, I didn't want to. 'Let it happen. Leave me out of it. It is too dangerous for me there. I will stay in my isolated bubble alone, cut off from everything and everyone, but at least I am not so much in danger here.'

At other times, particularly in the early stages of recovery, I would so completely retreat into my inner world that I had no knowledge whatsoever of what my body and conscious mind were doing, so was totally amnesic for the events that took place. I later learnt to gradually approach the outside world until I was more or less always aware of what was going on, even if I was not able to stay in control. This is a state known as 'co-consciousness'. I was in two places at once, in the bubble and yet in the present.

That sense of going back, away from the present, is sometimes known as 'depersonalisation'. It has been likened to being alone against a hostile universe and is the result of the desperation to create a situation in which you are in 'survival mode' and in which your perceived needs will be met.

The dynamic is believed to be very like that for an abused infant, only the danger for him or her is more than likely to be a real threat, not just a perceived one. So this way of coping works well for small children who are made to do things they don't want to do, see things they are not equipped to see or endure unspeakable atrocities. That retreating into an inside bubble, or safe place, becomes for them the primary coping mechanism for dealing with difficulties of all kinds.

The number of people coming forward with the symptoms of a dissociative disorder is rising. This implies there are more people in the general population who dissociate than previously thought. They have been so horribly abused or traumatised that their minds have fragmented in order to cope with the repugnant nature of what they experienced. It also suggests that the families into which the survivor was born were not providing the nurture and bonding that a small child desperately needs. An infant badly needs that nurture in order to be able to process and absorb stress-producing situations. It has been found that inadequate parenting plays a significant role in the formation of DID—the child has just not developed healthy coping strategies which are only formed when he or she bonds with the mother. This 'attachment', or connection, is vitally important for the infant's emotional development. The close, early relationship formed between baby and its mother is the glue that keeps the child bonded not just to its mother, but later it will determine the quality of all relationships with others and with itself.

Pippa didn't stand a chance of coping with her abuse any other way in the first place because something was wrong right from the start. Mummy was not a safe person for whatever reason. Perhaps she wasn't available to respond to her needs when Pippa was a tiny baby. That situation would have simply compounded Pippa's plight and made the creation of alters the only way to make sense of anything.

This is how one survivor describes DID:

> [DID] means missed days and weeks and for some of us even missed years; missed appointments, birthdays, holidays, weeks and weeks of missed school and work. It means embarrassment, sadness, humiliation, fear and, most of all, a lifetime of confusion. Once in a while, it can even mean some good times. But most importantly, it means survival . . . without it I and We would have died

long ago. [DID] is our shelter from the storms. (Jana D., quoted *from Multiple Personality from the Inside Out*)

Who? where? and what?

People like Pippa are not 'mentally sick'. However, they may have accompanying mental (and physical) illnesses which may, in this case, mean she could end up in the mental health system. It is hugely difficult to assess just how prevalent DID is in any population, though it appears right across the world. The International Society for the Study of Trauma and Dissociation (ISSTD) believes it is 'relatively common' (2011). Some studies have concluded that 1 to 3 per cent of the general population are dissociators, whereas others have quoted as much as 40 per cent. These discrepancies have to do with how you define DID and which group of people are studied (in-patients will have a higher proportion than the general population and certain classes and groups are more likely than others). According to one researcher, they are 'as common in the UK in fact as the hedgehog' (Karen Johnson 2012 from *Multiple Parts)*. The Sidran Institute states: 'It can therefore be placed amongst one of the four major health problems today, along with schizophrenia, depression and anxiety' (www.sidran.org). In one study carried out in an acute psychiatric unit in Norfolk 5 per cent of respondents had a high likelihood of DID, with a possible 22 per cent of those having a dissociative disorder. This is in line with studies undertaken in Canada, the USA and Norway (see www.dissociation.co.uk/research. htm).

One of the difficulties that need to be overcome in trying to assess how many in any one place suffer with DID is that it is a condition of hidden-ness. A survivor is highly unlikely to openly speak about her other parts (alters), never mind allow them to come out and speak—and one of the criteria for DID is that there exist 'two or more distinct identities' (Diagnostic and Statistical Manual IV). As one person with DID wrote: 'For most of us, we feel huge shame at having "parts" and do our best to hide them, letting them "out" as little as possible and only then in the safety and privacy of a therapy room or at home. And so many people will never get a diagnosis of DID because they refuse to be exposed in this way.'

Of course, it would be hugely helpful for every person with DID if it was better understood and that adequate funding was made available for research and treatment. 'Due to their link to early life stress in the form of childhood abuse and neglect, better recognition of dissociative disorders would be of historical value for all humanity including global awareness about and prevention of adverse childhood experiences and their lifelong clinical consequences' (Sar et al., 2011; see also www.pods-online. uk). However, much work is yet to be done and is being done. In the mental health field advances are being made and parliamentary debates are now taking place to explore what can be done to raise the profile of Satanic Ritual Abuse (SRA) and the accompanying symptoms of DID.

It is fairly typical for a person with a dissociative disorder to have been diagnosed with other mental illnesses, most commonly Borderline Personality Disorder or, if they have admitted to hearing voices, psychoses. Tragically, they are often hospitalised and treated for conditions they don't have, many times being medicated beyond their ability to think clearly or express what is really happening in their thoughts. However, *Pippa is not sick, she is hurting*.

Having said this, a survivor will often show evidence of other mental or physical illnesses which may mask the disorder or appear more pressing. This is understandable, given that a survivor's early life circumstances are not likely to have encouraged good lifestyle choices and practices and may also have caused physical and emotional damage outside of DID. People like Pippa may have spent time in destructive company, in sexually compromising relationships, or using street or prescription drugs to help deaden their emotional pain. This would inevitably lead to addictions, sexually transmitted diseases and harmful eating habits with unhealthy routines, behaviours and relationships.

People with a dissociative disorder may originally come to us struggling with insomnia or depression, or may think they are going crazy. They routinely forget small things, like where they have parked the car, or find articles in their wardrobe they don't remember buying. Some tell of hearing voices in their head, or of having headaches. (Headaches are often the result of inner conflict caused by alters vying for time 'out' or the opportunity to make a decision.)

Some survivors speak of being called by an unfamiliar name or being stopped and greeted by people they don't know. Others are prepared to admit that for years they have 'lost' time and 'come back' realising that it is minutes or hours, occasionally days, since they remember being in control of their life. Their spouse or partner may speak of them being moody or doing things out of character. (My husband would become frustrated when I vehemently denied saying or doing something that he knows full well that I had. He was relieved to find an explanation for that.)

Some people with a dissociative disorder are able to live fruitful, productive lives; in fact statistics show that the majority of people with DID possess above-average intelligence, are highly motivated, creative, are extremely sensitive and sometimes become successful professionals. Others may always struggle with mental or physical symptoms that necessitate prolonged stays in hospital or constant care in the mental health system. Accompanying psychosocial problems include material poverty, poor diet and inadequate housing which in turn lead to problems like obesity, diabetes, osteoporosis and so on. Other physical symptoms, which may be experienced as a result of the trauma, may include migraines, asthma and skin conditions, irritable bowel syndrome and related stomach ailments, and chronic fatigue. Insomnia is also often a big issue. With the lack of opportunities to make good life choices, some may also look for quick and drastic ways to cope with the inner pain including substance abuse, self-harm and eating disorders. All of these can be tackled and overcome. In fact, once a healthy mindset, plenty of support and stable lifestyle are established, many of the above issues resolve themselves. All of these issues can be addressed in the context of the Christian community, though it is important that other help is explored and not refused if appropriate.

The church is, rightfully, taking its place amongst those who are seen to be of help and who provide nurture to these survivors and there is reason for enormous optimism and expectation of real healing, given time and the right kind of help—and not solely inside the mental health system. We see the church as being the appropriate place for this to occur at every level, as informed and compassionate Christians boldly lead them to the truth. Philip Yancey has this to say: 'Where is God when it hurts? Where God's people are. Where misery is, there is the Messiah, and now on earth the Messiah takes form in the shape of the church. That's what the body of Christ means' (*What Good is God?*). Christians can therefore be sure that God will give them the courage to face the pain, knowing that their past experiences in no way affect who they are now as a redeemed and cleansed child of God. 'In him we have redemption through his blood, the forgiveness of sins, in accordance with the riches of God's grace that he lavished on us' (Ephesians 1:7-8).

Having come to some understanding of this incredibly sensitive and complex individual, we can move on into helping to create a safe environment for Pippa. She will need to feel safe physically, emotionally and spiritually if real and lasting healing is to even begin. The next chapter deals with the building blocks of that safety.

Chapter 5

DID—Shattered people

'The Lord is close to the broken-hearted and
saved those who are crushed in spirit.'
Psalm 34:18

'Blessed is the man who perseveres under trial, because
when he has stood the test he will receive the crown
of life that God has promised to all who love him.'
James 1:12

'All the world is full of suffering. It is also full of overcoming.'
Helen Keller

Finding a workable way to support a person struggling with DID, indeed with any long-term emotional problem, will be a challenge, but well worth the effort for the rewards it will give. But it is far better to have a plan in place than to simply field the crises as and when they crop up.

The survivor's needs may seem never ending. Valerie Sinason, a leading voice in this field, said in relation to abuse survivors, 'We can never be there enough' (quoted from a talk given on behalf of the Association of Christian Counsellors (ACC) Midlands in May 2009). It may sometimes feel as if we are never quite enough for the survivor, however hard we try, however much time and effort we give. Of course not, for it is not you that Pippa ultimately needs—you are only a reflection of the love from her heavenly Father that she is gasping for.

How on earth can we help?

But, we cry hopelessly, we just don't know anything about psychology, so how can we be of any help? We don't have to understand it all. We don't always understand why things work; sometimes it is just important to know that they do.

If you felt stressed you might have indulged in a relaxing brew and a piece of home-made chocolate cake, put your feet up, had a good laugh with a friend (or a good cry), and felt better. However, you may not understand the actual effect the warm liquid, the caffeine and the sugar had on your system, or the dynamics of laughter or tears to relieve pressure, or the release of feel-good hormones. But we do know that these things often work. They are not expensive. You cannot buy them in a bottle. They have been provided by God.

We may not understand how or why some things help in DID recovery in terms of physiology or psychology, but we can be sure that they do help. We are grateful for the knowledge and we can set about putting it into practice. We can understand that Jesus has the answers, that much of Pippa's pain can be alleviated as she both connects to Him and enjoys the love and acceptance that we, his Body, can give her.

In 1993 I returned from the US where I had been living apart from my husband and children while I received therapy. In Britain, however, I couldn't find anybody who was sympathetic to my condition (DID). I wrote to many well-known Christian counsellors and most said that this is a very rare condition and I would need a 'specialist'. As far as I could see, such people did not exist, at least not in my orbit. I broadened my search to the secular world—but with some trepidation, as I believed that many of the problems I faced had spiritual roots. I thought I may be completely discredited the moment I spoke of the demonic (I turned out to be right in that instance).

As it happened I did venture out of my comfort zone and eventually saw an NHS psychiatrist in a large London teaching hospital. I continued to see him for several months, in fact. He appeared to be fascinated by the symptoms I presented and the story I told. I faithfully reported in every three weeks, travelling by bus and train up to the big city to see him. He asked numerous questions and I was glad to at last be telling somebody what life was really like for me.

But my hopes for some effective treatment were to be dashed. I was asked to attend an evening meeting of young trainee psychiatrists and psychologists in order that they might observe an interview with me and then ask me questions. I agreed, naively assuming that as I was doing them a favour I would be well treated—after all, these were kind medics, who understood about trauma and distress. But it turned out that I was the monkey in the zoo, the performing bear, the spectacle. They seemed interested but sceptical. When the assault of personal, painful and insensitive questions about my abuse, my inner life, my memories and how I lived my life in the light of those, were over I was sent away. I had played my part well, they had received what they wanted and then I was dismissed. No one came outside the room with me; no one checked to see if I was OK. I felt humiliated and traumatised all over again. I sat on a hard seat in the empty, stark, echoing and dimly lit corridor and cried long and hard. The ordeal had completely drained me of any self-respect; my dignity was in tatters and I felt used all over again. I travelled home alone, on a dark, wet winter evening, catching three different trains filled with what seemed like hostile strangers, in a state of shock.

All I wanted at that time was to be accepted. I wanted someone to understand, someone to believe my story; not just what happened to me as a child, but what was happening in my mind every day, every minute—the voices, the unexplainable, the confusion. All I wanted was for somebody to believe that I could be well and free and OK. And I would go to any lengths to find it. That did not happen with these professionals. I was a phenomenon. In fact, from the very first meetings with this doctor I was warned not to dissociate in his presence at all, with the threat that if I did I would be locked up. My child alters, listening in from the inside, were terrified. But I kept going to the appointments because I held on to the hope that one day he, or somebody, would do or say something that would make it all better.

After about a year I decided to stop seeing him, even though there was no alternative support in place. I was on my own. (I did eventually find a caring counsellor who helped to contain the overwhelming feelings, but it was some years before I became free.)

Though hard to understand, that might explain why sometimes a survivor's commitment to her abusers is so fierce: 'I would let my mother abuse me every day if only she said she loved me' is something Pippa may well have said. To the small child, the desperate need to be accepted and loved by the most important people in the world—and later the small child within the adult—will dictate that she stays with them, often to the end.

As a free adult it is so important to give Pippa the message that her life doesn't belong to you or others, but to her alone (and ultimately to Christ). She may have felt indebted to others, a slave perhaps, all her life. Now she gets to reclaim her life and make choices. Pippa needs to understand, perhaps for the first time in her life, that she has options. She can choose the direction in which her life will go. The trouble with choices is that you take a risk and you may choose the wrong thing.

Pippa may, indeed, get it wrong occasionally. But these can be presented to her as opportunities to learn and grow, not danger zones. She can come to really understand that 'There is now no condemnation to those who are in Christ Jesus' (Romans 8:1), yes, even if she feels she has 'failed it wrong'.

A trail of pain

Trauma leaves behind a whole trail of symptoms: there's the depression with its irritability, loss of interest, loss of concentration, insomnia, hopelessness and sexual dysfunction, and then there's the numbing, the shame, self-loathing, nightmares, flashbacks, social anxiety, panic attacks, chronic pain . . . on and on the list goes. Negative thoughts rule. But 'a thought is just a theory, not a truth' (Dr Janina Fisher) and one of the joys of helping survivors like Pippa is watching the truth dawn, as she realises that she may indeed be wrong about the way she thinks of herself, the negative assumptions she has about herself and the world. Perhaps, just perhaps, there is another way to live.

There may well be times when Pippa is in crisis and we won't know what to do. It really is not our place to always know what is best for someone else, albeit a fragmented and hurting someone. Just as God can and does speak his wisdom to all who ask him (James 1:5), so he is able to give direction to Pippa herself and/or her alters. They will often be the source of their own wisdom when faced with a blockage.

It is good practice, each time we meet together, to ask Jesus to set the pace and to reveal what should happen next to Pippa and her alters. He will then direct the proceedings, usually revealing his will to Pippa rather than to you! We must try to resist the temptation to play God in her life. (We must also be careful not to spend all our time being too spiritual about this.) This bears repetition—we don't have to have all the answers.

The whole of the DID system is built to bring safety to the whole person and to maintain that safety. That is why the alters are so good at keeping secrets, even from the host personality. So, as long as we have taught the survivors who they now are in Christ, and how safe and secure they can be in him; as long as they understand that they have been told lies which they need to ditch in favour of the truth; as long as we are able to live lives of integrity and transparency before them and so demonstrate the reliability of our words, they will respond in the way that is best for them. We can trust God, and God-in-Pippa, for this.

Children

We need to be very careful when we identify a child who dissociates. Dissociation maintains some level of mental and emotional stability. Children dissociate in order to shield themselves from the huge onslaught of emotional pain that they are presently experiencing; to hold themselves together. It is unwise, even cruel, to try to dismantle the carefully constructed internal coping mechanism of small children. It may even put them in more physical danger. It is beyond the scope of this book to tackle the issue of helping abused children, but do take a look at the book list and helpful contacts in the appendices at the back.

Pippa comes to church
As Pippa, together with her internal family of other parts, grows up and moves away from her abusers, she will probably be physically safer. She may have taken an opportunity to escape involvement with the group, cult or coven. Abusers may have died, been incarcerated or moved away.

So let's assume Pippa ends up in our church. Perhaps we are on the ministry team or have befriended her on an Alpha course or in a cell group. She seems perfectly 'normal' until one day her fragile sense of safety is crushed and, and, like Natalie in chapter 2, she allows herself to 'fall apart' with those whom she sees as safe and trustworthy. We realise something has gone horribly wrong at some point in Pippa's life. We recognise that she is at a point when she could be a danger to herself and her struggles are beyond anything we have met before. She is showing odd behaviours and we suspect DID may hold the answers. But this is a huge discovery to make, and we may feel it is beyond us, as one survivor attested: 'I belong to a great and supportive church who, nonetheless, say that they haven't got time to release someone on the leadership team to work with me. This has left me desperately sad and torn . . . I can feel very lonely sometimes.' But there is a way to work with people like Pippa.

We will, therefore, need to find out more about this condition.

General facts about DID

History

The theme of fragmentation has been around since earliest times in myths and legends, including those of ancient Egypt in the stories of Isis and Osiris and the North American Indians in the myths surrounding Raven and the role, within their communities, of the circumpolar Shamans. In the nineteenth century much work was done in France and the US by Pierre Janet, William James, Morton Prince and Alfred Binet. Fragmentation of the personality was studied and recognised. (For a fuller explanation of these issues, see: Colin Ross, *Multiple Personality Disorder, Diagnoses, Clinical Features and Treatment*, Wiley-Interscience Publications,1989.)

Definition

Dissociative Identity Disorder is on the far end of the dissociative continuum. It is a highly sophisticated way of organising mental processes in order to avoid overwhelming pain. Put simply, it is a small child pretending to be someone else. It is also a wonderful, God-given coping mechanism.

In 1989 American psychiatrist Colin Ross wrote a significant book—*Multiple Personality Disorder*—as mentioned above. In it he writes that DID:

> embodies, in a profound and dramatic way, the struggle to maintain its integrity in the face of severe violation. That is a struggle in which we are all engaged to varying degrees . . . [DID] is not a curiosity or an incomprehensible aberration. It is a common-sense disorder, and its features are familiar from myth, legend, religion and literature. Many secular representations of (DID) aspects are found in our popular culture today, in comic books, movies, and elsewhere.

What DID is not

There are so many misconceptions around DID that it is worth knocking some of them on the head here and now. To begin with, **it is not an illness**. People do not need to be 'cured' of DID, nor do they need to take medication to make it better. At times it has appeared that people with this condition are immediately sent to the doctor, as if he could write a prescription and all would be well. In his book *More Than Survivors*, James Friesan, Californian psychologist and pastor, writes:

> MPD [DID] is not a disease. It results from dissociation, a God-given coping style that gifted children learn to use to protect themselves from the effects of serious traumas . . . People with [DID] do not deserve to be abused—they were able to deal with it creatively . . . These people are spectacular, but they keep getting presented to the public as damaged folk.

DID is not a thought disorder. In fact, far from being a 'disorder' it is more an 'order'; it is an amazing way of ordering the conscious mind to relegate the dark and harmful memories to a partitioned part so that life can go on untainted by distress.

It is certainly not incurable. If anything, it is the most curable of all the mental conditions. People with DID seem to be, on the whole, highly motivated towards recovery, often amazing their therapists and friends with their accomplishments. There is every hope that people with DID will fully recover, given the right environment, teaching and support. (Bear in mind, however, that other conditions which will also need to be addressed may exist alongside DID.)

People with a dissociative disorder are not mad or delusional, though it certainly feels as if you are going mad at times. Unfortunately, many are told that they are crazy, incurable or will need psychiatric treatment for the rest of their lives.

You can't catch it or even inherit it, though the ability to easily dissociate may be genetic.

It is not a creation of therapists or counsellors. It is not usually iatrogenic. It is, of course, possible that a therapist or someone caring for a survivor in some way may suggest certain ways of behaving which they may adopt. We are all influenced constantly by the people we spend our time with. But that can only be carried so far.

They are not making things up. The memories the survivors have are not fabrications, nor are they the result of watching too much television. It would be very difficult indeed for any individual to 'make up' the alters and then maintain them consistently over years. If they were able to do that convincingly they should be awarded an Oscar! However, people are still quick with accusations that they had pretended the symptoms for the purpose of 'attention-seeking'. There are plenty of other, much more effective methods of drawing attention to themselves, so why would anyone try to make up parts? It makes no sense and more often than not provokes disbelief anyway. In fact, attention is usually what the survivor does not want: DID is there to enable things to remain hidden rather than exposed.

So why is DID so frequently misdiagnosed? There are lots of very good reasons why doctors, mental health professionals and counsellors fail to pick it up. For some, it isn't even an option because they have either never heard of it, or assume it is so rare that it would be an unlikely diagnosis to come across. Others are sceptical of it being a bona fide condition, but rather somebody's carefully constructed excuse for bad behaviour.

There has been what professionals may call a 'low index of suspicion' among GPs and counsellors. If I had been born blind it would be almost impossible for me to truly understand sight. If I never dissociate, or even have that in my mind as a possibility, it would be very difficult for me to recognise and identify it in others. But the truth is we are learning all the time about how we function and it can now be on our list of 'indicators'—possibilities. Relatively few clinicians have come across DID because they have simply not been trained to recognise it.

Other disorders can co-exist, that is, exist alongside. Just because someone you know with DID also has dyslexia does not mean that all people with DID have dyslexia (or a stutter, or a learning disability or schizophrenia, etc.). Many of the other disorders can be identified and treated, but often the expectation is that the dissociative symptoms will go away once the treatment for the other disorder has been adjusted and administered. If they don't, and of course they won't, because it is a different condition altogether, the victim may be accused of not co-operating or medication may be changed or increased, or some other efforts made to tackle an illness the survivor does not have. Other diagnoses will be easier to diagnose and so be recognised in preference to dissociation.

One more thing to throw in the pot: DID mimics and overlaps with other disorders. If you look at the list of symptoms of DID on the next page you will see how many of them are shared with other disorders. People with DID almost always suffer from depression (understandable, given the background), but not all. (Depression also serves as a cushion to soften the blow against disappointment or to stem feelings of being overwhelmed.) Most dissociators are anxious. Once again, that is completely in keeping with their life history, but anxiety is only part of the picture. Sleep disturbance is often also part of the picture, as are eating problems, relationship difficulties, etc., the list goes on. But not everyone with these symptoms has DID and not everyone with DID has every one of these symptoms.

Even for clinicians who understand the nuances of dissociation, there are long periods when symptoms are hidden. The whole point of the splitting off of parts is to keep the truth of the abuse or trauma hidden from the rest of the world as well as from the host personality. Being hidden from the person themselves doesn't help when it comes to identifying it either. There are often very solid amnesic barriers in the way, for without them the survivors would not be able to function in their day to day lives. So when those barriers begin to crumble, and memory and awareness surface, their world may seem to disintegrate.

Each part on the inside seems to exist in isolation from the others, or at least it first appears to. Often this is not actually the case, and we may later discover a network of communication in the inside system.

Typical symptoms of DID1

Amnesia
A failure to improve
Multiple medical diagnoses
Severe headaches
Uncharacteristic behaviour
Unaccountable possessions and handwriting
The use of 'we' (speaking of themselves in the third person)
A history of trauma
Hearing voices
Sleep disturbances
Extreme indecision
Denial of actions seen by others
Mood changes
The obvious presence of alters

Symptoms that can cross diagnostic categories
(symptoms that are also seen in other disorders):

Depression

An urgency about time

A sense of extreme deprivation

The inappropriate need to please

A history of severe anxiety

Uneven school reports

Suicidal impulses

Self-mutilation and other forms of self-harm

Masochistic relationships

Alcohol or drug abuse

Eating disorders

Nightmares or sleep disturbances

Fears and phobias

Sexual difficulties

Auditory or visual hallucinations (seeing or hearing things that are not seen or heard by others)

The feeling of being controlled by outside forces

Secretiveness (the refusal to reveal personal experiences)

Flashbacks

Returning to Pippa, our fictional survivor—she is also likely to show high levels of intelligence, creativity, suggestibility and sensitivity. Without these skills she would not be able to have organised her mind into order and pattern. It is this order that has created and sustained the presence of her other parts and been able to use them to signal when danger is approaching and it is time to switch.

The feelings she will regularly experience will include a sense of utter abandonment, a sense that she is falling into a black hole, particularly at certain times of the day or the year. She may feel swamped in hopelessness and despair which results in a crushing loneliness. Because she had missed out on the early development of independence as a small child, but relied on her ability to quickly submit to the will of other, more powerful adults, she is likely to have no real sense of self, that feeling of being 'me'.

Amazingly, we are able to recover the identity that is unique to us. It is an absolute joy to develop that solid feeling that 'I am a person that is separate from you, and nobody is quite like me'—and really believe that that uniqueness is good, not something to hide and be ashamed of. 'I don't have to pretend to be what I am not, nor do I have to try to be like someone else.'

Such freedom is part of the liberty we are given as children of God: 'For you created me in my inmost being; you knit me together in my mother's womb . . . I am fearfully and wonderfully made . . . I was made in the secret place . . . All the days ordained for me were written in our book before one of them came to be' (Psalm 139:13-16). How amazing it is to be known and loved as special by the God who created the universe! Even the wonders of that creation have not yet been given what we have, that is, 'the glorious freedom of the children of God' (see Romans 8:20, 21).

So we understand DID, but how can the church help? Perhaps we need to understand what 'church' really is.

Chapter
6

CHURCH—Embraced
and understood

'The Spirit of the Sovereign Lord is on me,
because the Lord has anointed me to preach good news
to the poor . . . bind up the broken-hearted . . . proclaim
freedom for the captives and release from darkness
for the prisoners . . . to comfort all who mourn
and provide for those who grieve in Zion.'
Isaiah 61:1-3

'If we have no peace it is because we have
forgotten that we belong to each other.'
Mother Teresa

Church—the happening place

'I believe in the Church', wrote David Watson. So does God. In fact, he created the church so that Jesus could continue his works of grace and mercy on earth. That's where it all happens. The church—the Bride of Christ—survives throughout the ages because she is an extension of the works of Jesus himself, empowered as she is by the Holy Spirit. As John Stott says, 'the reason we are committed to the church is that God is' (*Through the Bible Through the Year*, Candle Books, 2006).

God has been in the business of healing the broken through his people for a very long time, long before anyone had ever heard of therapy or counselling.

It is time the church stepped forward once again, as she has in the past, to take her place as the leader in understanding and caring for those most hurt. Bill Hybels, a dynamic American preacher and author, said, 'The local church is the hope of the world. It's us or it's lights out.'

No pressure then . . .

However, we must be careful that we care in accordance with God's instructions, and not be too awestruck with the fashionable ways of thinking that modern psychology will throw our way. Some wonderful and helpful knowledge about the way our brains work, and how our minds cope with trauma, is emerging, but we will do well to continually measure it up with Biblical values and principles.

We have to be prepared to care for those whom the world may reject; to love those who appear unlovable; to forgive those whose acts have been what many regard as unforgivable. Philip Yancey again: 'All too often the Church holds up a mirror reflecting back the society around it, rather than a window revealing a different way' (*What's So Amazing About Grace?*). I wonder why it is that we are so bent on mirroring—copying—the world much of the time? We want to communicate in relevant ways, of course, but the people who are really searching are looking for an 'other' way, not the same way but wearing religious clothing.

Pippa's pitfalls

Church is not always a helpful place for Pippa and those like her. For starters, it is made up of people. One DID friend said to me, 'I don't find church very safe when people are in it. On my own or with people *who understand*—that's OK—it is only then I feel safe to worship and experience God.' Church has to be 'safe.' We will look more at safety in another chapter.

The more people understand the origins of DID the more they will appreciate the amazing way God equips our minds to overcome gruelling trauma. As her friends begin to understand where Pippa comes from, a kind of awe can emerge. Be careful, she is not an interesting phenomenon, she is a person. Faced with tortuous treatment, she has tapped into God-given mechanisms for survival. There is a danger that we will become indulgent or lenient. In our fervency to be the ones who now understand her, we set traps for ourselves. If we make her an exception we emphasise what she has felt all along: that she is different.

Regarding some wrong attitude or bitter thought that I didn't want to let go of, I was told too often, 'God won't ask that of you', or 'He knows your heart and that's what counts.' All along I knew what God says about the actions and attitudes I grappled with; I knew they were wrong and had no wish to be let off the hook. If concerned friends knew how unsatisfying, even unbiblical, those remarks are to a committed Christian—who just happens to have DID—they would be said less often. I want to know the truth too. My personal standards are as high as the next person's and I want to be able to trust my Christian friends enough to be honest with me. I have yet to meet a Christian with DID who wants to be indulged like a spoilt child.

It is certainly true that people with DID need and deserve time, patience and love but, as we saw in Chapter 3, that does not mean we turn a blind eye to wrong attitudes or what the Bible clearly states as sin. It is our job as compassionate and responsible carers, pastors and friends to help steer her through the maze of pitfalls in her thinking and behaviour. As she discovers who she really is in Christ, she is then able to acknowledge every part of her body and mind as being loved by God, and is accountable to Him. There is a clear place for repentance in any recovery journey.

God has given us plain instructions concerning our lifestyle, our relationships, our time and our affections. The Westminster Confession of Faith of 1647 says that 'the chief end of man is to glorify God and enjoy him forever'. Philip Greenslade puts it this way in his book, *Leadership*: 'To attain emotional wholeness is a fine aim, but we do well to set it just below a sight of God in all his glory as our chief ambition' (CWR, 2002). We must get our priorities right— whether whole or not.

Becoming like Jesus should be our goal. If personal healing is Pippa's only goal, when it appears not to be happening she will fall into the pit of despair. Healing can sometimes seem illusive, if not downright impossible, when in the midst of a long and painful trawl through old and painful memories and emotions. But if she realises that her life is woven into the beautiful tapestry of which you and I are a part, then the way she overcomes the trials of today has meaning in her life tomorrow. If her pain allows her to become refined like gold in a furnace, there is something good taking place.

Dazzled by God

Let's take a look at worship. People in pain, including those with DID, can still make the decision to worship—however they are feeling and whatever alters may be saying and doing. All the while we are able to make any decisions at all, we can decide to worship God. Of course, we are not to condemn or judge Pippa if worship is hard for her—and it almost certainly will be much of the time. In all likelihood there will be times when it feels impossible to worship at all, at least in a church setting. However, if we understand healing as getting our lives back into alignment with the way God intends us to live, it stands to reason that worship, and focusing on Jesus, can only do good.

'To worship is to quicken the conscience by the holiness of God, to feed the mind with the truth of God, to purge the imagination by the beauty of God, to open the heart to the love of God, to devote the will to the purpose of God.' So wrote William Temple. In short, it is all about being dazzled by God. But much of today's worship can be self-centred and subjective. We have a tendency at times to focus on what God has done for **me**: how he has healed me, saved me, had mercy on me. We sing about how much we love him, want him, need him; we ask him to fill us, equip us, empower us. However, true worship takes place not just in feeling and emotion, but in spirit and truth and those are the kind of worshippers God seeks (John 4:23). A sovereign God is able to intervene in our experience if he so chooses, but that is not what worship is all about.

Worship is more to do with being willing to respond in faith to God with pure adoration and in that comes the miracle of change. 'If worship does not change us', writes Richard Foster in his classic book, *Celebration of Discipline*, 'it has not been worship. To stand before the Holy One of eternity is to change'.

The declaration of who God is, who he has been throughout the ages and who he will be into eternity is our priority and our glory. That demands a decision on our part to worship him not just because he provides me with loving friends (though he does); not just because he has saved me from sin and hell (though he has); not just because he is preparing a place in heaven with him (though he is); but because he is the El Shaddai, God Almighty.

For Pippa as a Satanic Ritual Abuse victim there are many triggers in the context of worship. She may have a range of feelings in a church setting—immense pain, anger, terror—but not the 'right' ones, which she may see as being love, peace, gratitude. So in addition to everything else, she may struggle with guilt: 'I can't even "do church" right . . .' Apart from the possibility of flashbacks in the worship setting, the demands for an emotional response can feel very threatening.

How often do we encourage emotional responses, especially in charismatic worship and ministry times? There are invitations to come forward for prayer, or to receive anointing with oil or a fresh infilling of the Spirit. We sometimes put emotional pressure on each other. Some may find it a great blessing, but for others who perhaps do not function in that way, particularly those with abusive backgrounds, and even more so for those who have been ritually abused, it can be a very, very unpleasant experience.

Does that mean we stop encouraging responses in church? Of course not, but it does mean being aware of the provocative triggers it brings to alters, and are able to act rather than react.

Pippa's problems

Pippa will have more than one set of thoughts and inclinations. She has more than one part of her that functions in an emotional or cognitive way. Therefore, you could reasonably expect that she may have more than one response to, for example, the sense of God's presence, or a moving altar call. Emotional or mental overload is so common in church for a DID sufferer that it could almost be expected. She may also feel confused when a song focuses on our own response; it may feel that there are many, perhaps conflicting, responses going on inside her head. It may actually be easier for her to think about God than about her response to him.

Many times in the early days of my recovery I reacted negatively to something that took place during a time of worship. I have a vague awareness of running out of services in distress, of alters suddenly appearing feeling frightened and needing attention, even of collapsing over people. I am not proud of that though the leaders coped with sensitivity and kindness. But it must have been disturbing for the rest of the congregation. I am sure there is a better way.

Particularly in the acute stage of Pippa's recovery there is likely to be considerable 'leaking' of memories and feelings from one alter to another. If a committed Christian alter was watching the event (the alter would not necessarily be 'out'), the response of the host may be a positive one. On the other hand if, say, a teenage alter who hated going to church was watching, or an alter whose role it was to keep the peace by staying true to the cult or group, her reactions may be one of confusion, if not aggression. It can all be quite disturbing. She may have inside children who don't understand why they can't go to the front to watch the drummer, or who may want to suddenly go and sit with a safe friend on the other side of the church.

One alter I had, called Cherub, used to amuse herself by looking at other people's ears during the service and giggling, while J.C. would criticise the sermon constantly and Meg would have an enormous urge to run away. With all these mental gymnastics going on it is a wonder worship took place at all in my mind. Songs that state, 'I love you, Lord', or Bless the Lord, Oh my soul', can set off a tangle of inner conflicts, for who exactly is the 'I' can we are singing about, and how many 'souls' do we have? Just one, or one soul for each alter? And some of my parts may have no intention whatsoever of blessing the Lord.

To add to the turmoil, the host personality will almost certainly be suffering from a chronic lack of 'sense of self', and wonder who she really is. Once she comes to understand what is really going on the confusion subsides somewhat. I suspect the truth is, for most as it was for me, that it isn't until full integration takes place that worship in a corporate setting is completely hassle-free. I remember feeling great indignation that as the rest of the congregation seemed to enjoy the 'warm fuzzies' I sat feeling exposed and empty. When positive sensations in response to worship did come they felt unreal, dreamlike, as if they weren't really mine.

The popular 'I' songs can also provoke painful self-examination. There is a right time for that, of course, and for most people that should and does occur in church. But for the DID person it is potentially destabilising, especially if there are no adequate 'safety' measures in place. Nothing is simple for the multiple.

But as long as we are aware of the potential difficulties and have a plan in place, there is no reason why church services can't be a very beautiful and healing part of Pippa's life. Alters can learn to stay 'inside' until more suitable times are found for them to be 'out' and express themselves. It may be important to sit in a place in the back of church where she can slip outside for a breath of fresh air if necessary. There is nothing wrong with bringing a children's Bible to church, so that alters can look at that when they get bored or confused—though encourage an inner discipline to be developed whereby that wouldn't be necessary. However, at some stages of the journey alters may be more demanding so alternative measures need to be available.

Getting to grips with the Bible

Because our salvation is based on the fact of God's love and grace and has nothing to do with our behaviour, it is a good exercise for Pippa to be engaged in some form of Bible study that isn't connected with emotional or 'inner healing', but focused on who God is and what he has done in Christ. Then her thoughts will be centred on him and not on herself. Understanding that she is no longer a miserable sinner saved by grace, but a redeemed saint, all because of his works not hers, will be immensely liberating. Working through trauma can be hard work mentally and to give her mind a rest from the intensity of that will help to bring balance. I would also recommend simple stories with a Christian undertone. C.S. Lewis's *Chronicles of Narnia* carried me through a lot.

Everything in a dissociator's system will have great purpose. Nothing is haphazard or meaningless, however chaotic or strange it may seem. Some therapists put a great deal of importance on what is known as an ISH or 'Inner Self Helper': a particularly helpful alter who will know more about the inside system than any other. It may be important to make an ally of that part right at the outset. But don't worry if it is hard to pinpoint an 'ISH', labels are not important, it is enough to know that there will almost certainly be an alter who appears to know more than most and is able to act as mediator, peacemaker and decision-maker.

We must be cautious about looking for certain alters or having our own agenda when it comes to helping multiple alters attain freedom. God is well able to bring a person with a dissociative disorder into wholeness with or without the presence of any one therapist or counsellor. God has provided us with all the tools we need in order to heal and mature (2 Peter 1:3). If that were not the case, we must assume that traumatised individuals never became whole before psychiatrists and mental health professionals came on the scene, or in countries where these do not exist. That is not in line with what we know about God's love for all people and his ability to heal and save all who come to him.

We just don't know it all

Before we ever begin to seriously help someone with a dissociative disorder, we will have to honestly acknowledge that we don't have to have all the answers. *Of course* we don't know what to say and do in every situation. *Of course* we can't make Pippa better. In fact, the more we realise our own inability to 'fix' people with DID the better. We are not expected to do the healing—that is a matter between her and God.

Our job as helpers and carers is to facilitate their recovery journey. We can encourage, teach, guide and help to provide the safe environment which will aid recovery, but we must leave the big decisions of their lives to them. In this recovery journey we must not only be the teacher but also the pupil. We must allow them to teach us.

We may often find ourselves feeling completely out of our depth. We will feel powerless and won't know what to do. Pippa will know when that happens, however hard we try to bluff our way through. Survivors, particularly those who have developed dissociative abilities, will pick up every nuance, every change of facial expression, our eyes, and our body language. They will know when we are swinging by the seat of our pants, so don't even think about pretending you know when you don't. It is OK to be honest. The chances are she will know far more than we ever could about what is really going on inside and probably will also know what should be done. But her life experience and her low self-esteem means that she may not believe that she knows anything of value and will wait for us to come up with the answers. This is where we are firm—we must make sure she begins to trust herself and her inner instincts.

God has given each of us the ability to hear him in our own minds and hearts. By listening to her and helping her to listen to herself and all her parts, we can help her gain the confidence to hear God for herself. It won't help if we are panicky and anxious when it appears things are out of control. Just chill, stay cool, lean back on God. She will catch the current of peace and learn to flow with that.

Boundaries—flexible fences

There may well be times for Pippa when a child or particularly insecure alter, maybe Jimmy or Molly, will 'come out' uninvited or at an inappropriate time, or perhaps refuse to allow an adult alter or the host back into her body. In these situations it is important that we have previously worked-out boundaries. These are both to protect us and Pippa. She may not like these 'rules', or Jimmy may respond with anger or Molly with fear. Rules are scary when your childhood has been dominated by a complete lack of control over your choices—rules may be there to harm you. It may feel as if someone is governing her life all over again. But as she learns that freedom is something that occurs on the inside every bit as much as on the outside and that these boundary lines are safe ones (to keep the bad out as much as to keep the good in) the fear will reduce.

In 1953 Canvey Island, Essex, was flooded by the surge of sea water during a violent storm which claimed the lives of more than 300 people. In the wake of that disaster a massive new sea wall was built around the island which made it one of the safest parts of the UK from a flooding perspective. The houses on the front are no longer in danger of being flooded in the winter months. Now, strong sea walls protect the residents. Huge slabs of concrete were put in place to keep them safe from the dangers of the encroaching seas. Does that mean that they no longer appreciate the sea? No! But appropriate measures have been taken to keep dry land dry and restrict the water to the sea where it belongs. In other places flood barriers are in place which are only closed when flooding is a danger but would normally allow water to pass under them. These barriers are used as emergency measures, but are not usually required except when the tides are exceptionally high and the weather conditions dangerous.

Boundaries are like that—there are times when Pippa will need to contain any urge to switch until a more appropriate time and place, and the sea walls are permanently in place. There are also those barriers that are not in use until something forceful and potentially overwhelming occurs. Then appropriate times are made available for the alters to come out and release their long held pent-up emotions and memories. It is like a smoke detector which won't go off until smoke is in the air, at which times the alarm will sound and the sprinklers will set in motion. These boundaries are flexible in that we can choose to apply the right kind of discipline at appropriate times. This is not about taking captives, but more about putting up signposts.

Rules for behaving in church, for example, may be like the sea walls—some things will always need to be kept out. For some congregations, it may be right to protect them and the dissociator from any appearance of the alters. Some have the rule that no child alter is to come out in church. This is because other members of the congregation may not understand what is happening and may be alarmed or unsettled by an adult behaving in a childlike way. Keep in mind that Pippa may still belong to the church when she is a fully integrated and whole adult, so she will want to maintain credibility with her church family. But there may be other instances where 'coming out' is perfectly acceptable, perhaps in the home of a friend. Only if the alter at the friend's house becomes aggressive will the flood barriers need to be put into place and the boundaries strengthened. Those choices are about listening to God, to be wise and godly people, and not being stuck on hard and fast rules.

However, be careful about making exceptions to any boundaries which you put in place. Breaking your word, even if you see it as being particularly kind at the time, is showing Pippa that you cannot be trusted to carry through a promise. She will have learnt from an early age that people can change their minds at any point and that what seems good can, in fact, turn out to be very bad. Her trust in your reliability is weakened and you have proved that you don't follow through on your promises.

How then, can we as Pippa's friends and brothers and sisters in the Lord, effectively help her to move forwards into the healed and triumphant life that God means her to have? There is a way, because the New Testament teaches that in Christ we have so much: he has 'blessed us in the heavenly realms with every spiritual blessing in Christ' (Ephesians 1:3. See also 2 Peter 1:3, Philippians 4:13).

Chapter
7

TOGETHER—Loving in community

'May the God who gives endurance and encouragement
give you a spirit of unity among yourselves as you follow
Christ Jesus, so that with one heart and mouth you may
glorify the God and Father of our Lord Jesus Christ.'
Romans 15:5, 6

'If two of us were identical, one of
us would be unnecessary.'
Anon

I want to begin this chapter by quoting the Apostle Paul,
'Do not think of yourself more highly than you ought, but
rather think of yourself with sober judgement, in accordance
with the measure of faith God has given you. Just as each of
us has one body with many members, and these members
do not all have the same function, so in Christ we who are
many form one body, and each member belongs to all the
others. We have different gifts according to the grace given
us' (Romans 12: 3-6).

Pippa's longing for affirmation and love is acute, but it
is only as we work together that her needs can be effectively
addressed. Similarly, God is a mighty God, with a mighty
love to match and it is only as we love her together can we
even begin to convey that love.

Attachment

Here may be a good place to speak a bit about what is known as 'attachment' by mental health professionals. A helpful definition could be that attachment is a deep emotional bond that connects one person to another across time and space.

In the first few months of life a small baby in a healthy and functional family will form a deep and significant bond to its mother or primary carer. This bond will provide the bedrock upon which he/she builds its character, identity and view of life. It will be the secure base for exploring the world. This is the place he/she will go from and grow from, the point of reference as she develops. A good relationship means that a mother will respond to her baby appropriately and will instinctively know what is needed and be able to meet that need. The baby will return to its mother when things are distressing or frightening and that inclination will persist throughout childhood (and often well into adulthood).

The importance of this bonding is now not in dispute:

> The emotional bond that typically forms between infant and caregiver, usually a parent, not only stimulates brain growth but affects personality development and lifelong ability to form stable relationships. Neuroscientists now believe that attachment is such a primal need that there are networks of neurons in the brain dedicated to it. (www.psychologytoday.com)

Without that firm and stable relationship the infant is completely at sea. Without it she experiences a deep and lasting grief; a sense of deprivation; a longing that can become unbearable.

As a child abused from an early age by those closest to her, Pippa may have found the bond she had with her mother confusing. Sometimes she was comforting and nurturing, but sometimes she allowed harm to come to her. In fact that 'bond' was inadequate and did not provide the stability that was necessary for a healthy and robust view of the world to be formed. That caused Pippa distress and she had to adapt to a world within which she did not feel safe. Although she may have found substitute attachment figures later on, which went some way to fulfilling some of her needs, the lack of that early bonding will have affected relationships throughout her life.

Pippa was in many ways living in grief and lack, and so has stayed continually alert for signs of a stable mother figure somewhere in her life. Suppose that a group of kind and trustworthy people enters her life—her church cell group or support team. Supposing they begin to give her something of the compassion, affection and understanding that she has craved all her life. She might find that they willingly respond to her needs, often without her even having to tell them. One person in particular may have taken Pippa into her heart and home.

At this point, her deep and hidden yearning for that close attachment figure is awakened, and she may effectively 'fall in love' with that individual. After a while, it might feel to Pippa that she can't live without her and wants her presence all the time. She becomes distressed when separated from her for any length of time—much as a small child gets upset when parted from her mother. People begin to mutter that Pippa is depending on her friend too much and things become uncomfortable for the caring church member. At this point something quite tragic can happen— the caring friend may pull away in fear, overwhelmed by the intensity of the relationship. Pippa may then plunge into a deep, deep pit of despair as the long-hidden grief of rejection emerges and threatens to engulf her. It is a dangerous time for her as she struggles to restore some equilibrium, some reason to keep going, some stability, some sense of herself as an OK person. On the rebound she may swing back to old attachments, old relationships, even those which may have been abusive or harmful to her.

In the case of someone with DID like Pippa, her possessiveness may take many forms as different alters show their dependence needs, perhaps even pushing her friend away: 'I will reject you before you reject me, a situation I would not be able to bear.'

I remember a season of my life that was bleak. I had been admitted to hospital in California when I saw of video of an abortion procedure which triggered some early bad memories. I had collapsed with emotional overload and was kept in a psychiatric ward for several weeks. Cindy, whom I hardly knew and who had accompanied me to the hospital, had taken it upon herself to visit me early every morning before she started work. She was so kind, so gentle and seemed to really want to be there for me. I was deeply touched and in my vulnerable state responded eagerly. I so looked forward to Cindy's visits and after a while she starting taking me out at the weekends for a ride round town, or an ice-cream.

One Sunday she even took me to her church. But afterwards, she cut short our after-church coffee and chat and instead of the promised lunch treat, she suddenly said brusquely that she needed to take me back to the hospital. No explanations. She seemed angry—or anxious—I didn't know which. I was distraught. What had I done wrong? She seemed in a hurry to get rid of me. On leaving me at the hospital she said she wouldn't be able to visit again. I was not to phone or try to contact her in any way; that that was the end of the relationship. I couldn't understand what dreadful thing I had done to cause this sudden rejection, and later went over the morning's events endlessly, trying to find an explanation. In a daze of grief, I entered the ward and cried until there were no more tears. I wept for a week, almost it seems without a break. I was inconsolable. It seemed crazy to have such a reaction to someone I had known no more than about five weeks. I didn't want to eat or sleep. All I wanted was to see Cindy again. I did try to phone her but she had changed her phone number, so driving the message home even further—you are not wanted here. You are bad.

I had become attached to Cindy and she had, for a brief time, become the mother figure I so desperately wanted. However, her own needs had got the better of her. Something must have triggered her in the service, or maybe something someone said to her, and in her anxiety around commitment she panicked, so had to push me away rather violently. Two people trying to survive. Two people with unmet needs.

This happens all the time in our relationships with hurting people like Pippa. Like I was. Suppose we could dilute that dependency, spread the load in a way that is manageable to all concerned. The truth is that Pippa will have to go through that period of attachment; she will have to face those burning needs for attention, affection, nurture—love. She will have to work through separation anxieties too. It is both painful and overwhelming, but in that raw and tender state, Pippa will be able to access the reality of what was and what could be. She must be able to see what is missing, acknowledge it, understand it and then choose a way of filling those needs with the all-encompassing healing and comfort of God. But the halfway house transitioning from one state to the next has to be an attachment to people who can offer her something of what she has missed. A team of people rather than just one person—whether it is a close friend or family member, a counsellor or therapist, or a pastoral figure—works much, much better. It is together that we represent God in all his aspects and together we can lead Pippa to understanding the companionship of Christ, the encouragement and empowering of the Holy Spirit and the awesome and glorious presence of an Almighty Father God.

We will be examining how we can form this team later in the chapter.

Support structures
'Alone we can do so little, together we can do so much' (Helen Keller). Given that the Christian life was never meant to be lived in isolation, if any people need to feel embraced and loved by a community, then it's those with DID. As the Heart for Truth ministry testifies, it is imperative that people

like Pippa are made a part of a small 'family' or group of friends who know and love them—and know and love each other. Each one of these friends will have a different—and distinctive—role in the healing journey. Jesus Christ is very definitely the centre of the circle which is solution (Christ) centred not problem (troubled person) centred. There is unity and equality amongst the members of the team, of which the troubled person is simply another member.

So, this is not a picture of Pippa being in the middle of a circle of do-gooders, feeling embarrassed or perhaps over-important. She is part of a circle of loving friends— saints of God—and Jesus Christ is undisputedly the focus of attention. Within this circle there is complete confidentiality, so although nothing goes outside of the group, information and concerns about Pippa's welfare are shared with one another, with her full knowledge and consent. Although Pippa is the reason this group is set up in the first place, she is not only on the receiving end. She has work to do. Pippa will be giving to the group just as she is receiving from them, and she also works to understand herself better, and to move forwards in her spiritual and emotional maturity.

Truth Teams

We in Heart for Truth call these groups of loving friends 'Truth Teams'. The reason for that name is that the central task of the team is to assist Pippa in every way to understand the truth of who she is and what God has done for her in Christ. Each member of the team has a role, according to the gifts God has given—just as in the church—and they use these in the Truth Team to help Pippa grasp the truth. She will probably believe some hefty lies about herself, God and the world. If she didn't there would be no need for alters to keep the pain from overwhelming her. In fact, if she really believed the truth, there would be no pain that she could not handle.

The motto for the team, which is applied both the Pippa and to other team members is: **'You alone can do it but you can't do it alone.'** Pippa, in spite of the appalling abuses she has had to suffer, *really can* move on into wholeness; the team members *really can* lead her into that place. The only reason that we can claim that with any certainty is because we have been given that promise, which is more than a bunch of nice-sounding words, but is the truth: 'I can do everything in Christ who gives me strength' (Philippians 4:13).

Having a team within which Pippa can learn and grow does not just help Pippa herself. The rest of the team will be on a journey of discovery too. It is not about feeling sorry for someone and trying to help them. It is about discovering the gifts God has given each of us for the good of his Body; it is about learning how to pray when things are overwhelming; it is about working together as a team. Most importantly it is about coming to God together with the hurting person, realising that we are all wounded, all in need of God as he is revealed in each other. (So this team approach applies to any needy person, not just those with DID.)

Every member of the team only does that which God has anointed them for—so we don't try to play the serious counsellor if we are really the team clown (you may, of course, be both!). One may be in a position to spend hours listening to Pippa's stories of inner and pain and memories of abuse, another may only be able to pray with her after the morning service. One may walk the dog with her every Saturday morning and someone else may share Sunday lunch with her once a month. But in every activity the truth is spoken and lies exposed and renounced.

Within this framework of 'micro-church' or family, Pippa, with Molly and Jimmy and any other parts, begin to feel that they belong, that they are valued and respected, and they have been created by God to do more than just survive. In time, the security Pippa feels will sink down throughout her system, the Word of God takes root, and peace takes the place of fear.

Truth Teams also provide much needed support for family members of a DID survivor. A schoolteacher friend,

Gareth, and his DID wife were supported by a Truth Team. He writes:

> My wife Sophie now has fellowship with trusted women in her Truth Team, who have kept faith with her even through times of regression. She is learning to trust again, and we both have support, prayer and compassion in times of stress. Most of all, Sophie has the reinforcement of key truths. It all assists the process of her re-education. I am so grateful to the Team.

When another multiple, who was unable to read the Bible because of the reaction of her alters, was finally able to freely read the scriptures, one pastoral worker wrote: 'Without . . . the Truth Team we wouldn't be where we are now. I can't believe this could happen without someone going to some specialists!'.

Truth Teams

When a church is supporting someone with DID or some other severe trauma-based difficulty, one of two counsellors or carers will not be enough. The survivor will require support in every area of her life.

A Truth Team is a group who will be there to look at all levels of need, both practical and spiritual. What's more, it is to help positively—and with confrontation where necessary—in the process of kicking out the lies and enabling the survivor to believe the truth, so much so that it changes the way she/he lives their life.

When DID has been the primary coping method, alters are able to feel that there is enough strength in their support network to handle the extremes of need they present, in both behaviour and traumatic memory material. Therefore they can afford to relax inwardly, allow each alter to emerge and say what needs to be said, and all remain in a place of being held securely in the strong and flexible embrace of a whole group of trustworthy people.

The task of a Truth Team is first and foremost to direct the process of transforming and renewing the mind of the person who is troubled—and at the same time finding that their own ways of living and thinking have become renewed and God-inspired.

The team may consist of maybe only three or four, or as many as ten or twelve. It means the struggling person is surrounded by clearly defined strength in Christ. It is a resource that he/she can call upon and even contribute to. This is not an exercise in mollycoddling.

The wounded person will need to:

- want to be well and move on in God, believing that the key to their freedom lies with faith in Jesus Christ, lived out in His Body
- be prepared to submit to the process and trust the support team.

Team members must:

- know who they are in Christ
- understand the principle of personal responsibility
- be prepared to work together as a team
- be aware of and acknowledge their own gifts and ministries
- be aware of and acknowledge their own weaknesses and limitations
- understand—and are comfortable in—their specific role in the team.

Connecting the fragments of church

Church is not 'easy': 'to dwell above with the saints we love: that will be glory. But to live below with the saints we know— that's quite another story' (source unknown).

Churches that are unwilling or unable to attend to the needs of troubled people will not, indeed cannot, be whole. Because we are all wounded in some respect, and because we all need to acknowledge our need of a healing Saviour, by denying our frailty we are denying our need of God in Christ. That body of people will be incomplete, fragmented, as each member tries to appear more whole than they are. How can they be completely united, knit together as one, if each member only sees another according to their limited and false self-disclosure? God's blessing cannot be fully released: 'How good and pleasant it is when brothers live together in unity! . . . For there the Lord bestows his blessing, even life forevermore' (Psalm 133:1-3).

If church is not 'safe', then we will not be comfortable enough to be honest and transparent. We will create a false church, the pots of coloured paint we spoke of in relation to integration will stay separate, in their own cans, locked and lidded. That church is a divided and fragmented one. Only as we can allow ourselves to be vulnerable, and accept each other unconditionally, with or without other 'parts', with or without recognised gifts and ministries, with or without the social graces we come to expect from each other, can God really move in unfettered power amongst us.

'May the God who gives endurance and encouragement give you a spirit of unity among yourselves as you follow Christ Jesus, so that with one heart and mouth you may glorify the God and Father of our Lord Jesus Christ. Accept one another, then, just as Christ accepted you, in order to bring praise to God' (Romans 15: 5-7).

So also in that same attitude can we see Pippa begin to bravely accept the truth that she is loved and protected by God and that you embrace all of her, alters included, as one in Christ. He can and will bring her to a place of wholeness and freedom, as you walk with her, together, in the jangle of conflicts and unity that make up our daily living-out of the Christian life. Truth Teams are simply a structured way of beginning this process.

Nothing worthwhile is ever easy

We cannot, however, say that this is an easy road. It was never meant to be, there are adversaries at every turn. John Ortberg puts it like this:

> How high a value would you say God places on making sure people who follow him lead comfortable lives? It seems that God wants to use us, wants to grow us up, and wants us to be strong and wise and courageous. He doesn't appear to be terribly interested in making sure we're comfortable. He would not make a good flight attendant.
> *When the Game is Over it All Goes Back in the Box*

Helping Pippa to gain an understanding of who she is as a child of God in such a way that her inner, troubled parts feel comfortable and able to hand over to Pippa the control they have had in her life, is not easy. But it is immensely rewarding. Ultimately it is about watching a flower unfold in the sun; about giving the Holy Spirit opportunity to unlock chains that have chaffed and burned and imprisoned someone for a long time. It is the story of Isaiah 61: 'to release the captives' and watch as the grieving ones become 'Oaks of Righteousness'.

Chapter 8

SAFETY—A place called home

'In peace I will both lie down and sleep for you
alone, O Lord, make me dwell in safety.'
Psalm 4:8

'The ache for home lives in all of us. The safe place
where we can go as we are and not be questioned.'
Maya Angelou

Having understood what we are working with, we can move on to practicalities. How can we provide an environment within which Pippa can heal? A most important factor to grasp is that Pippa will feel much more able to look at what is happening in her mind, and face what has to be faced, when she feels safe and secure. A Truth Team could provide a helpful structure for the suggestions below, but is not the only way. God is able to use whatever we offer him.

When I was in America there were times when I just did not know where I would sleep or how I was going to find the money to buy food. It wasn't until I had the certainty of a roof over my head that I was able to make significant progress in working with issues of the past. When I knew at the end of the day that I could go to a place I called 'home', however temporary it was, it was easier to focus on deeper things.

The search for home

We are wired to need that 'home': that earliest of major influences, the setting in which we are bonded to significant people and which continues to be the model of safety and relaxation. Without that, every alter or part will need to continue to exist, to provide protection and safety in the absence of any other source of emotional shelter.

Rosie's story

One lady with DID, whom we will call Rosie, was feeling really unstable and the whole of her life was chaotic. Her children were struggling in school and the school was struggling with her children. Her husband was at the end of his rope and her church didn't know where to turn next. Rosie herself just couldn't understand what was going on and why the voices in her head were so loud and the memories of the past were emerging and flooding her mind. Nowhere was safe except her bathroom where Rosie retreated for some kind of peace, though even here she knew unrest and turmoil.

I had the privilege of teaching Rosie, her husband, her church friends and leaders about DID. We looked at what it is and how we, as people of love and integrity, can help in her recovery journey. Because of that, home and church became a safer place, one in which she found a measure of understanding, privacy and shelter from the demands of life. She also learnt more about what was going on in her mind and body and why, and consequently she felt safer and able to relax. Then she was in a better place to look at her horrible memories and how her alters had been created to deal with past abuse. That sense of being understood, and of now being safely held, changed everything. Within a few months she had integrated all her alters and could start to think about the rest of her life. She is now a successful nurse and her beautiful children are blossoming under her fun and creative guidance. Those at church are delighted and continue to be inspired by her confidence and joy.

Everyone is different and each person's healing journey requires a different timespan, but the truth is the same. While you and I cannot invite Pippa to live with us (although occasionally that is the right thing to do), we can facilitate that sense of her being in a good place.

Basic needs, basic safety

There is no point whatsoever in spending lots of time praying for Pippa and ministering to 'the needs of her soul' unless her basic needs are met. Straight talking James speaks with great clarity about the need for Christians to walk the walk as well as talk the talk. 'Faith by itself, if it is not accompanied by action, is dead' (see James 2:15-17). If we want to see struggling survivors come through into healing we will need to put in the time and the energy. And yes, that does mean sacrifices on our part.

To really see transformation in our congregations, our churches have to be seen as 'safe'; every survivor needs a safe environment in which to heal. When I walked in the Peak District with my daughter one chilly March afternoon I remember remarking on how easily startled the sheep were as we approached. They would stop feeding, lift their heads and watch warily before scattering from us. No feeding resumed until we were at a safe distance. All their instincts tell the sensitive sheep that relaxing (and for them that includes eating) is not on the agenda until they can be sure that all is well.

As God's sheep, we cannot 'feed' from the good things that give us spiritual nourishment—teaching, prayer or fellowship—unless we feel some level of safety. In order for hurting people in our Christian communities to find that nourishment in God, we have to make sure they are not looking around them for danger. I don't mean that they will be expecting someone to leap out and cosh them while they are drinking their after-service coffee, but I do mean that they may not be able to fully relax inside themselves, happy that the people around them mean them no harm, criticism or judgement until they are in a good place in every way.

We can divide safety into two camps: the safety in the physical world in which we live—safety on the outside, and the safety in their minds—safety on the inside. The information which follows does not just apply to those who have DID, or even to people who are struggling in any way, but to all of us. It is included here because we sometimes neglect the obvious or mundane issues in our pursuit of some 'special' rules or advice, when all the time the keys lie in the things we already know.

Safety on the outside
Let's take a look at the kind of things that help us feel safe on the outside. First, there are the basic requirements we need for life:

The importance of feeling full
'He satisfies the thirsty and fills the hungry with good things' (Psalm 107:8).

We can become a little tired of the media emphasising again and again about how and what we should eat. 'You are what you eat' we hear, and there is ample evidence in nutritional research that our bodies and minds are far better equipped for the rigours of modern life if we pay close attention to what we do and don't put into our bodies. Keeping ourselves fit and healthy is not a new idea. The Jews in the Old Testament five thousand years ago had rules for healthy eating and palaeontologists tell us that doctors in ancient India, China and Indonesia used to treat diseases mainly by altering the food habits of their patients.

So if we know what it is that keeps us in peak physical and mental condition, doesn't it make sense to particularly apply that to those who are traumatised? Not all out-of-control behaviour has its roots in mental or emotional distress. Many symptoms of apparent 'demonic activity' or emotional dysfunction would be set right if Pippa were to cut down on the junk and eat fresh, wholesome food in the right amounts when she needs it (which generally speaking is three or four times a day). There is so much evidence that books are awash with it. Children who eat breakfast perform better at school; students attain better results in academic and behavioural tests if e-numbers are eliminated; prison inmates are less aggressive when served fresh, organic fruit and vegetables in place of fast-food alternatives.

When my husband and children returned to England and left me alone in America to finish off my therapy, we estimated that I would rejoin them in a couple of months. (However, it was to be three and a half years before I saw them again.) I initially stayed in the home of some friends. They worked all day leaving me alone in the house. I didn't have a car and having no transport in California really does curb what you do (catching the bus wasn't an option—there weren't any). To add to my restrictions, I had no money and no prospect of any—as an 'illegal alien' I was not entitled to any kind of unemployment payment.

I was hungry. My hosts had a full fridge—in fact, I had never in my life seen such a large fridge or one packed so full with goodies. They had told me I could help myself to anything I liked. I didn't. Even though I was achingly empty I felt uncomfortable about taking things that weren't mine, especially as I hadn't even earned it. I didn't deserve 'freebies'. Very occasionally I made a frugal sandwich, but felt ill at ease in doing so, and even then was very economical with the fillings. This was in contrast to my friends whose sandwiches were huge and bulging. The less I ate, the less it felt that I needed to and my energy levels plummeted with my weight. It left me lethargic and depressed. I can see now how irresponsible I was in not looking after myself and this only contributed to my emotional decline.

How I wish then that somebody knew what was happening and could have spoken to me about grace. God was graciously offering me, through these Christian people, an answer to my need. It would have been altogether right and appropriate to have gratefully received it. Being hungry is really no fun and a depleted physical state has repercussions in every other area of life. At times it was assumed I was being hassled by demons and therefore was prayed for at great length, when all the time my extreme behaviour was more to do with a low blood sugar level than anything more sinister. My caring friends had no idea that I had only eaten for some dry bread early that morning.

Let's apply those principles to our abuse survivor. There may be good reasons why Pippa is not eating as she should. We may think that diet is too obvious to be even worth mentioning, but we often misunderstand its importance in the recovery process. What we eat affects our energy levels and our mood. Diet affects our serotonin levels, which is a 'feel-good' hormone, and in the long term it can prevent or bring on serious disease.

Shelter and sanctuary
'The Lord . . . blesses the home of the righteous' (Proverbs 3:33).

Shelter is the second basic need, but a need that is perhaps not so easily met. If Pippa does not live in warm, safe, private and comfortable surroundings, she will not be able to deal with spiritual and emotional issues adequately. If she is living next to the 'neighbours from hell', however much prayer and counselling she gets she will not feel safe enough to begin to absorb all the good that is being offered. Does her roof leak? Has the heater broken down? Can she afford to pay the rent or the mortgage? Is she in an area she is comfortable with or does she feel unsafe even walking down the street?

Pippa is particularly vulnerable to being triggered into overreacting, or switching (into other alters or parts) by stressors that we might take in our stride. We may have to support her as she seeks different accommodation so that she is strong enough to tackle difficult internal issues.

Really real relationships
'Do not be yoked together with unbelievers . . . for we are the temple of the living God' (2 Corinthians 6:14-16).

However much she works on her emotional issues, if Pippa then goes back into an abusive relationship, or spends time with old friends whose habits and lifestyles are harmful, we won't see much progress. It may be that it is Molly, the alter who is driven to please the cult or group, that draws Pippa back into harmful places or with dangerous people. That will need to be addressed. It is one thing to work on believing the truth, but if we then go back into an environment in which lies are thrown at us continually, we are doing ourselves no favours.

This issue is sometimes the most difficult for survivors to tackle. Pippa may have to leave the area and start again somewhere else—maybe Molly is completely hoodwinked through a form of mind programming and need to put distance between herself and the abusers. This is particularly true for Satanic Ritual Abuse survivors who may continue to be contacted by the group in which they were abused. This can be a hugely important but immensely difficult issue, requiring sensitive and wise advice. Having good, loyal and kind friends is a good start to understanding the value of real friendship and will help Pippa to discern which relationships are destructive.

Also, we tend to become like the people we spend our time with, so the question can be put to her: who would you want to become like? Plutarch once said, 'If you live with a lame man, you will learn to limp.' We are influenced enormously by those surrounding us every day.

Rest and relaxation
'There remains, then, a Sabbath rest for the people of God . . . let us therefore, make every effort to enter that rest' (Hebrew 4:9-11).

Nobody performs well if they are tired. Sleep is vital to our well-being and so we do well to adjust our lifestyles to include the right amount of sleep, which for most of us is between seven and nine hours a night. It is highly likely that most people with DID will have had sleep problems at least at some point, some having suffered years of insomnia. God intends us to sleep during the hours of darkness and be awake and alert during the hours of daylight. It is a pattern that has worked for mankind since Adam and Eve, and it is only since the invention of the electric light that we have taken control of the natural cycle of day and night and abused it, resulting in a range of physical and mental problems. Of course, it is right and good that life goes on during the night and many jobs and professions depend upon it. However, a healthy lifestyle means to live within the cycle of life that God has put in place. So we must make sure Pippa understands how to structure her daily routines to facilitate adequate rest and sleep. Occasionally, sleep aids from the GP are just the thing to facilitate the re-establishment of good sleep hygiene—healthy sleep patterns.

Working at working

'Make it your ambition . . . to work with your hands . . . so that you will not be dependent on anybody' (I Thessalonians 4:11).

God intends us to work and there is a great deal of satisfaction and fulfilment to be had by working regularly, not to mention the good it gives to society at large. Most people with DID will be unable to work during the critical stage of recovery, but it is still important to take a look at how their time is being spent. A routine of work and play, the chance to lose themselves in focused and pleasurable activity, is so important. To have the opportunity to regularly concentrate on something other than their inner journey, or the voices within, is paramount to keeping a strong mind and good mood. We all need to spend some time each day in occupation in which 'time flies' and we are not aware of the passage of time, or of time 'weighing heavily' upon us.

The best way of engaging in this is to do something creative, using the part of our brain (the frontal lobe) that develops our inventive, joyful, beauty-making skills. Once again we are falling back into line with God's intentions for us and that can only bring goodness and health to both our minds and our bodies. It is also important to look at Pippa's week and check that her time has some routine, some rhythm to it, that she knows what she will be doing at various points in her week, that she has some pegs upon which to hang the things she may have to do.

For example, if she helps in the charity shop on a Monday afternoon and sees her pastor or counsellor for a deeper chat on Wednesdays and always goes to the women's group on a Thursday morning, she has the bare-bones of a structure to her life. Church on Sunday could be the highlight, a place where the 'dots are joined' and many of the significant people in her life are worshipping together. She can then fit in doctor's appointments, babysitting or whatever. If she is able to work the issue may be about how she spends her evenings and how and when she relaxes and winds down.

Contentment
'Godliness with contentment is great gain' (1 Timothy 6:6).

'Contentment makes poor men rich; discontent makes rich men poor', wrote Benjamin Franklin. Children who have lived in a state of perpetual alertness, waiting the next onslaught of abuse, learn to stay aroused and never really relax. For years that 'hyper' state is maintained, so the idea of completely 'chilling out' takes a bit of getting used to. To find herself in a situation in which there is no obvious outer danger, and in which all her physical needs are met, is a very good starting point for Pippa in the lesson of peace. Paul had it: 'I know what it is to be in need, and I know what it is to have plenty. I have learnt the secret of being content in any and every situation, whether well fed or hungry, whether living in plenty or in want. I can do all things through him who gives me strength' (Philippians 4:12-13). Notice that Paul was content in plenty as well as in want! We usually take note of it being the other way around. Also notice that contentment came just before Paul spoke of being able to do all things through Christ. There is a link there: contentment brings with it resilience and inner stability which helps us cope with challenge.

Survivors of extreme abuse are sometimes more ill at ease when things are looking good than when they are not! 'Deprivation I know about, abundance I don't—What's the catch? Who's trying to trick me?'

Personal devotions and fellowship
'They devoted themselves to the Apostles' teaching and to the fellowship, to the breaking of bread and to prayer' (Acts 2:42).

We must encourage Pippa to do what we do (there's a challenge here)—have a consistent routine of Bible reading and prayer. Regular attendance in church and/or a midweek meeting is something that should and probably will come as a result of your working with them. Obviously if Pippa was abused within a religious setting (not at all unusual), then extra support and patience will be asked of us, her friends. Perhaps Molly is very antagonistic to the church and its activities and this causes inner turmoil. But nothing is too difficult for God and Pippa can expect the gradual calm and balm of his Spirit to reassure her that real, true worship of the living, loving God is not only safe but healing. That reassurance will eventually reach Molly and she may need to confront her fears—again, safe relationships are so key here.

There is no end of online information, teaching DVDs, television programmes that will teach Pippa and her alters about God and his love and expand her understanding—though we need to be discerning. We recommend the Freedom in Christ materials as exceptionally faith-building and non-threatening (see the contact details at the back).

This cannot be stressed too much, especially to those who support the wounded. There is no substitute to actually knowing the Word of God. It is life-giving by its own admission. There is so much power in his Word—in fact it was by his Word that the world was created right at the beginning and his Word continues to create that which is good. 'In the beginning was the Word, and the Word was with God, and the Word was God . . . The Word became flesh and made his dwelling among us' (John 1:1, 14).

Wounded people are no exception—they too will be renewed and re-created as they feed on the Bible. In fact they are particularly hungry and thirsty for that which only God can provide. We are all invited: 'Come, all you who are thirsty, come to the waters; and you who have no money, come, buy and eat!' (Isaiah 55:1). God freely satisfies our needs and gives us the ability to live by his word. J.B. Philips said that while he was translating the New Testament he felt like an electrician working on the wiring of a house with the power on! 'The Word of God is living and active, sharper than any double-edged sword' (Hebrews 4:12).

Pippa is vulnerable and weak, she has gone through a lot and feels frightened and fragile. She cannot handle life on her own. But she doesn't have to, God has provided a way for her to live and the instructions are all in the Bible. It really does work.

I make no apology for stating the absolute importance of helping chaotic, confused, angry or 'messed up' people to get to grips with what God is saying to them. At the risk of sounding like a nineteenth-century preacher, we have to boldly announce the power embedded in the Bible. The Stoics used to say that the only way to live was 'sub specie aeternitatis', that is, 'under the shadow of eternity'. If we can help Pippa to see herself as part of a much greater picture in which she can play a vital part, meaning and purpose will begin to emerge for her.

Instead of grovelling down there in the emotional gutter with the survivor, why not gently coax the hurting person up to our place, seated with Christ in the heavenly places? More on that later, but let's make sure we always have one eye on eternity in all our dealings with Pippa, Molly, Jimmy and all her inner parts and, of course, with each other.

So Pippa is now in a place of outer safety. It may be important for her to move house, away from abusive family or relatives. Or change from a stressful job. Or move churches. Her mental stability, her future, her very life could be at stake, so also the lives of any children or dependants. This is not being overdramatic; these dangers may still be present and very loud in her life. They must be addressed.

Safety on the inside
Having established outer safety in a sound environment with good people around her, good food inside her and a daily structure for living that gives at least the hint of fulfilment to come, we will need to introduce to Pippa a new way of thinking.

Like all of us, Pippa needs to know that she is not in danger of having life taken from her. Survivors are often still fighting when the war is over—still battling for their lives when they are no longer in danger. The fact that alters are present tells us this. But Jesus has already won that battle. Inside safety—the understanding that nothing can change my status as a loved and valuable person—is the really big issue. Once Pippa come to grips with this, it can change her life for ever.

1. Know who and whose she is
The colossal mountain for Pippa to climb is to know who she is in Christ. Unless we begin to grasp the truth of who we are as a redeemed child of God, we will continue to live according to who we think we are and that may be not much at all. Arguably, the most important aspect of Pippa's healing is to have a solid sense of identity—who she is as opposed to what she does, where she comes from or where she is going. Trying to grasp the truth that she is loved can take a long time and require a lot of patience when every experience in her early life has been geared to telling her that she is evil or worthless. But helping any wounded person to find his or her identity in Christ is so very important to their progress. For the person like Pippa who has been so badly hurt that their mind has splintered, this is of profound importance.

'Belinda', whom I met in London, grew up believing she was 'trash'. Everything she ever did she assumed was worthless. Even though she gained a good degree in classics and was a beautiful and accomplished young woman, Belinda's inner voices and her whole experience of life bought into the lie she was given at an early age, the lie that said, 'I am worthless, and everything I do is rubbish.' It is not surprising then, that by her late twenties she had to abandon her husband and small son. Not only could Belinda not live with herself, she couldn't live with others either. Living with the knowledge that her life had no worth became almost unbearable and all her coping mechanisms broke down. How could any of us live out the victorious Christian life when that kind of lie is rooted in your being? You can't. The lie has to go.

Working on believing the truth and kicking out the lies will take the rest of our lives, so making a start and focusing on God's Word can't begin soon enough. We will look at another four areas in which we can help Pippa to create that stable basis upon which she can build the rest of her life.

2. Resolve spiritual conflicts

Issues preventing Pippa from connecting with God will need to be tackled. One important solution for her long-term healing, peace and maturity will be to understand the principles of forgiveness. It will be vital for Pippa to forgive everyone with whom she has an issue. It must be quickly said that this need not be as daunting or as unreasonably demanding as it sounds. Forgiveness is not forgetting what happened—that would be impossible for her. Neither is it condoning the dreadful abuse and saying that it doesn't matter. It certainly does matter that she was harmed so cruelly. Forgiveness is saying that she is prepared to let go of it all and allow God to deal with those who hurt her. Holding on to anger and resentment, cradling a desire to take revenge on those who are responsible for her pain, is absolutely understandable but not at all helpful for her. In fact bitterness will only prolong the distress and feed the cancer of unhappiness and bondage. Pippa will need our constant encouragement that forgiveness is something she can do however hard it may feel. The benefits are life-changing.

Other issues will emerge as we get to know Pippa. There may be things on her mind that she will need to ask God's forgiveness for, attitudes which she knows are wrong. There may be things she will want to renounce, to turn her back on and announce her faith in a God who makes us clean. Knowing you are pure before God is an amazing feeling after years of living with a deep sense of your own dirtiness.

3. Know who to trust

'The moments that matter most in our lives are not fantastic or grand. They are the moments when we touch one another' (Jack Kornfield).

Another item on Pippa's list of inside safety measures is to know who she can trust. Any survivor of abuse will be unsure of those who are and who are not trustworthy. That is completely understandable, of course. In the past she has been betrayed by the very closest of people, those who should have been there for her—in many cases the protectors became the perpetrators. So Pippa may fall into one of two camps. She may either trust no one, not allowing herself to come close enough to be known and loved, or she may have such unsteady boundaries that she entrusts herself—and probably her body—to anyone who appears to offer some affection, or who promises to meet a perceived need.

It is vital for our peace of mind that we are sure of the people around us. Suspicion breeds suspicion and survivors who cannot trust others often become themselves untrustworthy. They may also give the message: 'I don't trust you. Keep away from me'—not the best way to 'win friends and influence people'. Trust is a key component to survival and we need to get that clear in our minds. Within the church we should find the most trustworthy people on earth.

3. Know your strengths and skills

What are her strengths and skills? This may seem a little premature when she is still thinking about survival, but building upon the good things she is starting to recognise in her life will increase her self-esteem. That, in turn, will help to give her hope for the future, which will lead to developing personal goals and purpose. When Pippa can say, 'I know who I am, I know where I have come from and I know where I am going', she is well on the way to being complete in Christ. That sense of inner stability will seep through to the whole system of alters and give them the feeling of safety. That will enable them to come 'out' where necessary and share what needs to be shared (if we have provided her with appropriate people to hear and respond with wisdom and compassion).

4. Know your goals and purpose

Once Pippa has acknowledged her strengths and has been encouraged to build on them, she will be able to formulate a goal, a dream and a purpose and ultimately will be able to recognise God's calling. Even in the midst of her panic and the crazy thoughts and feelings that may be surfacing, especially as she is now recognising and interacting with Molly, Jimmy and other alters, she will with our help, still be able to promote the positive things in her life. God has plans for her future and we can be a channel for that hope and expectancy. We must speak to her about her dreams and goals and help her to discover what she does want as well as what she does not.

> 'For I know the plans I have for you', declares the Lord, 'plans to prosper you and not to harm you, plans to give you hope and a future. Then you will call upon me and come and pray to me, and I will listen to you. You will seek me and find me when you seek me with all your heart. I will be found by you,' declares the Lord, 'and will bring you back from captivity.'
> Jeremiah 29:11-14

Chapter 9

ALTERS—Protective parts

'For you created my inmost being; you knit me together
in my mother's womb. I praise you because I am
fearfully and wonderfully made; your works
are wonderful, I know that full well.'
Psalm 139:13, 14

'If we could sell our experiences for what
they cost us, we'd all be millionaires.'
Abigail Van Buren

Mapping the system
When we first meet someone with DID we often think to
ourselves 'Help! What on earth do I do now?' It helps, as
counsellor, friend or carer, to know exactly who it is we
are working with—who is actually on the inside of Pippa.
Without this knowledge we end up making guesses about
what's going on. Believe me, our guess is more likely to be
wrong than right. Pippa herself also needs to be comfortable
that she has some understanding of what is going on inside
her head and why. A really good start is for her to draw a
'map', a diagram or picture, of who is on the inside system
of alters or parts.

Everyone's map will look different and is unique
to them. For example, my map consisted of a series of
balloons, each one representing an alter. Some were
grouped together around a particularly dominant alter and
some were more isolated. For example, J.C. was a loud and

bolshie fourteen-year-old alter who carried much of my anger. She fought for justice and became extremely angry if she perceived any unfairness in my/our life or in the lives of those close to us. Nobody messed with J.C.! Around her 'balloon' were grouped Stormie, Beckie, Honesty and Panda, each carrying a specific aspect of anger or memory of injustice.

I knew one young woman whose alters lived, in her mind, on a seashore. Some were together in a series of beach huts, some were in trees, one or two were alone on the beach and some further inland. Another DID lady drew the picture of a house when asked to illustrate how her inner system worked. There were alters who occupied the dark attic, others were in more accessible places like the kitchen or the living room, even the entrance hall. The ones who felt shame more deeply and did not want to be easily found hid in the cellar.

It is amazing how organised and ordered these systems are; even if to the uninitiated it may appear chaotic. Trauma creates changes in the brain. 'Our brains are sculpted by our early experiences. Maltreatment is a chisel that shapes a brain to contend with strife, but at the cost of deep, enduring wounds' (Martin H. Teicher, *Wounds that Time Won't Heal*, www.danafoundation.org, 2000).

> Once viewed as genetically programmed, the brain is now known to be plastic, an organ moulded by both genes and experience throughout life. A single traumatic experience can alter an adult's brain: A horrifying battle, for instance, may induce the flashbacks, depression and hair-trigger response of PTSD. And researchers are finding that abuse and neglect early in life can have even more devastating consequences, tangling both the chemistry and the architecture of children's brains and leaving them at risk for drug abuse, teen pregnancy and psychiatric problems later in life.

The biology of soul murder: Fear can harm a child's brain. Is it reversible? US News and World Report, 11 November 1996

The brain will naturally try to bring order, that's how God made us. It will also seek to bring meaning, even out of harmful experiences. Neglect, trauma and shaming will all confuse and dis-order neural networks, leading to what seems to be a dysfunctional system whereby so many networks remain unintegrated. Connections that should be made are not made. Conditioned fear will continue to prevent integration. So Pippa's brain, in trying to establish order, will have created her own organisation; hence the system of alters who interact and who hold separate and managed responsibilities.

Drawing an internal map can be an enlightening and releasing exercise for the person with DID and can satisfy her need for control. It can also serve to explain her other 'parts' to those journeying with her. As recovery progresses, the map will change—some alters will be added as the system feels safe enough to reveal them and some will be taken off as alters feel safe enough to integrate. We will look more about integration in Chapter 13.

Working on her map could become be a regular task for Pippa as she charts her recovery progress and it is a way of being able to share the daily victories with others. Pippa, or even Molly or Jimmy, may like to show you her map, say, once a week or once a month. It may be used as a springboard for talking about what is going on in her inner world: who is feeling afraid or bold, or who needs to talk about some sensitive issue or memory.

Naming the alters

Everyone is different and each DID person will refer to their inside parts in different ways. In her book, *When Rabbit Howls*, Truddi Chase wrote an account of her own personal exploration of who she was as a multiple. She called her inside people 'the troops'. Other names I have come across include: 'The Others', 'Little people', 'Littlies', 'Munchkins', 'The children'. In most books they will be referred to as 'Alters'. It is important that they choose their own collective name as they also choose individual names. Some people with DID don't have names at all for their alters, but I would suggest that they might like to give names to the key players; it is simply easier to have a working relationship with them if there is some form of identification.

The reason for not having a name may be as straightforward as just not thinking of one, or as complex as not feeling worthy of a name. While we would not want to major on relationship with any particular alter apart from any other, we do need to convey to them, right at the beginning, that they are each of great worth and value and equally so. It is also important that they come to understand that each alter is part of one whole person and as such are equally significant in what they contribute to the functioning of the whole.

Pippa's got work to do

In order for Pippa to truly know that she is loved, she will need to be able to expose the whole of her being, including and especially her alters, to God. To help her in that, we will need to take another look at Pippa's inside system of alters. Why are they there? Do they still need to be there? What do they do? How can we make God's love available to them when they are so afraid?

Bear in mind that as a helper—a spouse, friend, pastor or counsellor—all you can do is to provide safety, structure and support. Most of the work is done by Pippa herself, not by professionals or prayer counsellors. The hard work is theirs to do. We simply cannot heal Pippa, though we may dearly want to. Alison Morgan in her book *The Wild Gospel* says, 'We can easily become a bubble protection agency rather than a bubble bursting one, ministering compassionately to the oppressed but stopping far short of setting them free' (Monarch, 2004).

Our job is not to 'protect her bubble'. We don't just want to see Pippa coping with life any more, as amazing that those coping strategies are, because 'the glory of God is a human being fully alive' (Iranaeus). That means supporting her through the bad times as well as the good in that journey towards becoming 'fully alive'.

Why alters were created

Each alter will have been created at a time of extreme and overwhelming emotional overload. The pain, which may have been physical as well as mental, would have been beyond what a small child could bear. So in our example, Pippa created Molly and Jimmy. In my own life, I created JuJu and Stormie, J.C. and Meg, Elliot and Skye, April, Pieces, Cherub, Jude, Whisper, Panda, Secret and many others. Each had a specific reason for coming into being.

Reasons for the creation of alters would fall roughly into two categories: either an alter personality was created to hold a specific memory or group of memories (I had an alter who held all the memories associated with a particular uncle, for example), or an alter was created to contain an emotion which seemed to threaten their balance and emotional stability. Either way, they were created to take something that the core personality of the child was unable to hold, in order that they could still be functional.

Hiding bad memories from the core personality will enable the child to live a somewhat 'normal' existence, giving her the ability to behave in a way that keeps her from standing out in a crowd. There will be a protective wall of amnesia between the alter and the core—Pippa just would not have any recollection of what happened when Jimmy came and took over her consciousness: a blessed escape for her at the time.

The whole point of DID is to keep the truth of the abuse hidden from view, to hide the dividedness. In most cases abused children are warned not to tell 'the secret' or they will be harshly punished. For example, I was told that the 'bomb' planted in me would explode if I ever told anyone of my experiences. Those who have been abused in a ritualistic way, and/or in a satanic coven, might have been threatened that telling the secret will result in other children being treated even worse than they themselves have.

There would have been no escape for the abused child other than the escape inside him/herself. So it will have been understood that it is in their best interests to keep their head down, to be quiet and 'be good'. One of my alters, during therapy sessions, would tremble while whimpering of how she promises to be quiet. When abused as a child I was ordered to be quiet and still and then everything would be alright. But however hard I tried to be still and quiet (and that is very hard when bad things are happening to you), it never was 'alright'. But still that faint hope was there—if only we could be still enough or quiet enough . . . It was to become a major goal of my life, to be a 'good girl' and therefore the title of my autobiography, Am I A Good Girl Yet? (Monarch, 2005; rev. edn. AuthorHouse, 2012). It is so important for the abused child to be as unnoticed as possible. Those reactions may continue well into adulthood, influencing her choices and shaping her personality. I was a quiet and rather secretive person right up until my thirties. I learnt how to cover my tracks and to be unobtrusive, silent and invisible. I would move around the house at night—I have always suffered from insomnia—and leave neither sound nor any other evidence that I had been there.

How ingenious to be able to create a whole set of separate parts who know the truth of the abuse but can hide it from the child that has to function in the everyday world! That is cool—that is clever—that is a 'God thing'!

Wrong ways of seeing alters
In the mid nineties there was a doctor in the Midlands who saw alters as ego-dystonic (not a part of you but outside of yourself) and 'aliens'. He believed that the presence of alters inhibit and obstruct healthy and pure growth, that they are the cause of all the grief and hardship and therefore have to be eliminated. He maintained that if we get rid of the

alters, then all negative and overwhelming feelings, habits and weaknesses will also go. Therefore alters are to be killed off, murdered, pushed off cliffs, shot, taken to heaven or somehow obliterated, so that the 'real' person can live. I visited him and was shaking badly after the interview. He taught that conventional therapeutic interventions are no good whatever and are to be shunned and disregarded. (I was left wondering what kind of damage that did to vulnerable and hurting people who had already grown up thinking that they were bad and evil.)

This approach would confirm a Christian survivor's worst fears, but is, in fact, a complete lie. There is nothing bad about being a survivor; as a Christian she is God's forgiven and cleansed child, loved and totally acceptable to him. It is as impossible to 'get rid' of alters as it is to rid yourself of your brain. They are a vital part of who you are.

Some alters will hold memories of the most horrific abuse but not be able to also contain the emotion that accompanied it (that will be the task of other alters). An alter may be able to recount ghastly events without showing any appropriate emotion. Their particular 'personality' would not have developed that ability. Others hold emotion but may be unreliable when recounting the events, as their 'memory' will consist simply of feeling the feelings. Emotions such as extreme rage, disgust, acute embarrassment or paralysing terror are difficult for a young child to deal with and so the existence of another part to hold them makes life more bearable. Alters can embody, for example, denial or anxiety but they may be unable to fully explain why they feel those things because the complete memory of the accompanying traumatic event may reside in another part. Pippa's alter, Molly, may speak openly about her mind-blowingly cruel treatment in a ritual without showing an ounce of distress, but at some other time Jimmy, or another alter, may come out who is so broken with tears and grief that he/she is almost unable to speak, but may not be able to give a reason for her emotions.

At times during my recovery I would be overcome with terror. My five-year-old alter, JuJu, would come 'out' (she was originally created to hold fear) and would be absolutely terrified, but unable to give any credible reason why. She would walk round in circles in the office of Christopher, my therapist, not knowing where to turn or what to do to find a peace. The explanation would be held by someone else. All she would be able to say is 'I will be good, I will be good' in a high-pitched voice and it would take Christopher a fair bit of detective work to figure out the reason for such fear.

So, given that alters are created to contain and hold something that the whole person perceives as being harmful or threatening the sanity or survival of the 'core personality', once the threat has gone the alters are no longer needed. At least that is the logic of it, but convincing the whole system of that can be quite a challenge.

Child alters

There are virtually always child alters present in someone's dissociated system; in fact, sometimes there are no adults at all represented. That is not surprising as the offending trauma will have happened—or at least begun—at a very young age. The alters are frozen aspects of themselves, unable to mature as the years go by.

Child alters are to be treated in age-appropriate ways, using language and allegory which they will understand. The person concerned is not play-acting. Neither is she trying to get attention by pretending to be a small child. It is even more than regression. The presenting alter really is only at that age and stage. Age, in this context, is not to do with time, but with maturity.

Gentleness, kindness and unconditional acceptance for who they are works best when speaking to a frightened child alter, however incongruous they may appear. I have worked with the child alters of all manner of people. One day I was sitting in church with Paula who had switched into her six-year-old male alter called Tommy. He was crying with fear and misery (he had not yet figured that he was in a safe place and that no one was going to hurt him). Tommy leant on me as we sat at the back, unobserved by the rest of the congregation, and sniffed into my shoulder. All was well until he decided he wanted to go forward for prayer. I hadn't realised he was listening to and understanding the invitation from the front. Not wanting to deny him the opportunity to feel loved I agreed, in whispers, to take him down to the front. He held tightly onto my hand as he rushed forward down the aisle, still sniffing loudly, tears still rolling down his very red cheeks.

Tommy had the language, actions and understanding of a small child though 'he' dwelt in the body of a 43-year-old woman. Bear in mind that Paula was almost six feet tall and rather, let's say, buxom. I was four feet nine-and-a-half inches high (still am) and weighed six-and-a-half stone (no longer). Now, how would you explain that relationship to questioners afterwards? I learnt a few lessons that day—and some members of the church gained more knowledge than they had bargained for.

Bearing these things in mind, speaking to Pippa's alters sensitively will serve to build on the sense of safety we are creating. Be aware that other alters may be watching what we say and do 'from the inside', testing our integrity and trustworthiness. They, like all abuse survivors, will be hypersensitive to any change in outward circumstances or inconsistency in our words or actions. They will notice, for example, if a chair in our room is moved, if we are wearing a different watch or if we fail to greet them in the familiar way. They may pick up if we are in a grumpy mood, or feel particularly tired, angry or preoccupied. They are likely, however, to assume it is their fault.

Some alters may appear to be very, very authentic, as indeed, they are. But they are *not* full personalities. There is only one personality (hence the change from the title 'Multiple Personality Disorder' to 'Dissociative Identity Disorder'). While we make sure the basic needs of each alter are met, it will not be helpful to indulge every whim, or to give too much attention to each individual alter. While tempting to favour endearing child alters, playing with them and showering on them the love and affection they have so obviously lacked, lots of time in play may achieve little more than cementing the dividedness. Rather, it is better to acknowledge their need and help them to discover, *as a whole,* how they can find those needs met initially within themselves and ultimately in Christ. Bear in mind **that it is the whole person that has the need**, the alter is simply expressing it.

But it is certainly important that we praise each alter for the contribution they have made to the survival of the whole person and for their part in the overall achievements of the core.

One day Mandy came to see me when I was working from home. She was brought by a friend who had stood by her over many years of unexplainable problems. Mandy had fairly recently been diagnosed with DID. She was clearly feeling insecure in a strange place as she sat on the edge of my sofa. As we talked together, exploring ways in which she could be supported in the long term by her local church and other Christian friends, she became unhappy and agitated.

As Mandy was obviously quite comfortable with me, I shared that I understood that she had other parts inside and spoke gently into her inner system. I invited anyone from the 'inside', who may need to speak to me about that idea, to come out. One of her alters, a teenage boy, appeared and wanted to check me out. He was rather sulky, complaining about my lounge and particularly unimpressed with my battered old TV. He was also suspicious of my intentions. Why would they have to let anyone else know about them? Aren't they OK as they are?

After introducing myself I asked him if he minded if some of Mandy's friends came to know just how well he had protected her and how he had persevered all these years in a thankless task. I told him that if a few safe people were taught a little about him and Mandy they would appreciate just what a brilliant job he had done in helping her. He warmed easily to that idea, asking more questions, which I answered as frankly as I could. When Mandy 'came back' she appeared to have a complete change of heart about enlarging the circle of friends who knew about her difficulties, even though she was completely amnesic to the conversation I had had with her teenage alter.

In addition to child alters, there are almost always alters whose job it is to be protective, in which case they can be aggressive. These may come out when the core personality feels attacked in any way. This could include times of prayer (particularly, it appears, during 'deliverance' prayer). They can be a major source of concern to those trying to help, as often they appear to be sabotaging the healing process. It helps to understand that they are simply doing their job, the one for which they were created: to prevent other people from knowing too much. They have not yet understood that all is now safe and that the core person will come to no harm if she knows the secrets of past abuse or the inside system. So the theme of safety must be revisited again and again.

How to recognise a switch

What does this actually look like? You may be speaking to Pippa but she may appear not to be listening. She may look a bit glazed, or perhaps stare into space. She may flutter her eyes, or close them. She may even keel over and become what looks like unconscious for a short time, perhaps a few seconds. Then Pippa will look at you in a different way, perhaps more shyly or coyly or angrily. Her facial expressions may not seem in character, perhaps older or younger; perhaps more aggressive or more self-assured. When she speaks her voice may seem different—more gruff or higher. You will know that there is something about her that is not in keeping with the 'old Pippa' that you know. It is at this point that you may like to say something like: 'Hi, I wonder who this is. I don't think we have met before. Do you know who I am?' Always be welcoming, however angry the alter may appear. An alter usually comes out for a reason—often because they have something to say, or communicate that is important to them. Be prepared to listen carefully and with respect and give them honour as a part of someone you know and love.

We don't have to entertain the alter or feel we have to be anything other than ourselves. The chances are they have been watching you 'from the inside' for some time anyway—their knowledge of you will be greater than your knowledge of her/him.

You may like to ask the new alter what their name is and why they were created in Pippa and ask if there is anything they would like to say to you or ask you. When it feels as though the alter has said enough, you could suggest that Pippa comes back, unless there is anyone else who would like to come out and speak.

Why do alters come out?

So what is it that makes alters 'come out'? How is it that a person with DID can spend lots of time in one place and appear as normal as everyone else and yet in another place, with other people, she can switch into other personae? As I see it, there are two main reasons why an alter will come out in these circumstances. The first is that they respond to what some clinicians used to call a 'negative hook'. That is, they are forced to come to take over control because life situations become scarily like the original, traumatising ones. So, of course, the alter created to deal with fear, say, will come when potentially frightening situations arise. The host is not equipped to deal with fear, but a specific alter will be.

During a particularly dark time when I was living in California, I was placed in a psychiatric hospital that was unfamiliar to me. On the first day I was not quite sure what I was allowed to do and what I wasn't. Even though I had spent time in mental health wards before, this one was new to me and had a different set of rules. Unwittingly I strayed into a corridor that was out of bounds, and an overzealous nurse became frustrated and cross with me. She found me just at the point where a long and deserted corridor went round a sharp bend and I was literally cornered by her. I was in a state of anxiety already (that was why I was there in the first place). The realisation that I was lost and couldn't find my way back to my room simply accentuated my anxiety. The nurse was obviously angry and her anger was the last straw. I had tried so hard to be 'good' but I just wasn't good enough, it seemed. By her annoyance the irate nurse took me beyond what my coping mechanisms would allow and JuJu came out.

JuJu was created to handle my fear, particularly fear brought on by the perception that I had done something wrong. As she stood up (for I would temporarily lose consciousness before I switched and fall to the ground) she cowered before the nurse, trembling, apologising in a high, whining voice. (At that point in my recovery I was co-conscious for much of JuJu's appearances.) The nurse was furious and ordered me to stop behaving like a child, saying, 'These tactics don't work in here.' The trouble was, her reaction produced even more fear, which made it doubly impossible for me to return to my adult self. If she wanted me, the adult, to take control she would need to reduce my fear levels and calmly reassure JuJu that all will be OK. She didn't know that, of course, and as her demands became more and more angry poor JuJu could only protest meekly that she would 'try to be good'. Only much later, when the nurse gave up in disgust and marched me back to my room (which is what I was looking for in the first place) was JuJu able to calm down and allow me to regain control. That was a negative hook at work.

The second reason an alter will come out is a much more controlled one—the person with DID feels safe enough to relax and allow herself to be whom she needs to be at that moment. That is a 'positive hook', such as in Mandy's situation described above. Mandy recognised that I understood and she allowed her teenage alter to come and talk to me. This is not likely to happen with Pippa until we have gained her trust and she feels as though she has, in us, an ally who is on her side.

I was always ready to switch when I went to see Steve Goss and the Freedom in Christ team—these are the people who first introduced me to the way of believing the truth that set me on the road to complete freedom. I felt utterly safe with them. All the alters on the inside wanted to come and express themselves; they instinctively knew that these were

OK people. We always met in a neutral, quiet place, with no chance of being interrupted or spied upon. JuJu vied for time out with Stormie, a twelve-year-old alter (one of the angry ones who had mellowed and become secure and stable) and with Cherub, who was a six-year-old alter.

In these circumstances we may have to watch that alters don't just stay out because they like to be in our presence. As satisfying as it is to have them feel secure and welcome, it is important to remember that each alter is only a part of the whole person and that the goal is to see them integrated and united. So once they have received the warmth and understanding they all crave and have expressed what they needed to, try to encourage them to allow the host or core personality to return. Cherub was often so glad to be out that she made sure all eyes were on her and it was sometimes very difficult indeed to persuade her to allow my core personality back.

One time JuJu was intent on staying out when Christopher was trying to speak to all the alters about integration—not a popular concept to my fragmented self at the time. JuJu was determined to remain out, so she talked about jam sandwiches, new shoes—anything to keep Christopher engaged with her rather than follow his plan of spending time with someone else. He had to be quite firm in the end and his tone of voice was enough to show JuJu he meant business. In that case her trust of Christopher was such that she was not hurt by his authority and she eventually went back inside.

As Pippa's alters come and make themselves known, in the atmosphere of acceptance of who they are and the job they have done in keeping the core personality protected, so the next part of this healing process can develop. We have gained an understanding of the inside picture by mapping, and we understand the ongoing task of meeting those alters who need to, want to and are happy to come out to speak or communicate with us. The next point to reach is for us to be available to listen to the disturbing memories of trauma.

Chapter
10

MEMORIES—Windows
of understanding

'Be careful that you do not forget the Lord, who
brought you out of Egypt, out of the land of slavery.'
Deuteronomy 6:12

'Have I not commanded you? Be strong and courageous.
Do not be terrified; do not be discouraged, for the
Lord your God will be with you wherever you go.'
Joshua 1:9

'The past is a foreign country, they
do things differently there.'
L.P. Hartley

There is a school of thought that says all the memories of
all the alters need to be expressed, sifted through, reframed
and dealt with before integration can even be contemplated.
Although a perfectly logical progression, this is often felt not
to be the case. Note that it is not the traumatic event or
events that have caused the real damage, but primarily it is
the message taken from it that has caused the woundedness
and fear: 'I am damaged goods; therefore I am only of
worth in as far as I can be of use to others.' Centuries ago,
the Greek Stoic philosopher Epictetus wrote: 'People are not
disturbed by experiences but by their perception of those
experiences.' It is how we see things that determine how we

124

react to them and it is in *knowing* the truth that we are set free (John 8:32).

However hard, we can do it

We therefore need to understand the part that memory plays in both the causing of injury and woundedness, and in recovery. Memory is set in the context of a mind which has been taught certain things about what is right and what is wrong, what is seen to be true and what is understood to be untrue. This is the raw material we have to work with and sometimes we have to work hard to sift through the jumble of false perceptions before we hold an ordered and God's-eye-view of the world. But however hard, it can be done.

Whatever the difficulty, every person also has resources they can use to help them tackle and cope with those difficulties, albeit with the help and support of caring people. In 1 Corinthians 10:13 Paul wrote about temptations: 'God is faithful; he will not let you be tempted beyond what you can bear . . . he will also provide a way out so that you can stand up under it.' The Message Bible puts the second part like this: 'All you need to remember is that God will never let you down; he'll never let you be pushed past your limit; he'll always be there to help you come through it.' There is always a way. That applies to us all, including the most damaged and hurting Christian.

Even people with severe mental illness have healthy areas of their lives and we need to help them discover and nurture these. For most, the 'ill parts' of their lives are far outweighed by the 'well parts', it is just that self-image and world views that are negative have overwhelmed them and prevented the good stuff from being recognised and utilised.

Lessons we learn, about who we are, before the age of about four or five become the bedrock upon which we build our world view. If I was loved, I learnt and continue to believe that I am of great worth and so can live with confidence and security. If I was neglected or ignored, I learnt and continue to believe that I am of little significance or value and so live with low self-worth. If I was hurt or abused, I learnt and continue to believe that I am bad and deserve punishment and so live with self-loathing.

So, early lessons in life may not be based on the truth as we find it in Jesus. Clearly, those who have been so badly abused that they have resorted to extreme forms of dissociation in order to survive will not have received true and good messages about who they are. Instead they have been 'taught' lies—for instance, that they are of no value apart from what they can give sexually or for use as a servant or plaything. These lies will need to be replaced with the truth if they are to know real freedom (John 8:31, 32). In fact, once the lies are no longer in place, the alters won't need to be separate; their job will be done and they can choose to integrate and become one with the host personality.

We could include within the framework of truth our own truth. My psychologist in California, Dr Christopher Rosik, writes:

> Might it also be possible that each one of us are . . . called to become increasingly aware of our own personal truth, including the aspects of our childhoods that may have been too painful to acknowledge or remember at the time? If genuine healing only occurs in the light of a conscious awareness of truth, then it seems possible to understand the prolonged healing process as an expression of God's gracious care. (*Am I A Good Girl Yet?*, Monarch, 2005, Appendix A)

While telling the whole story may not be the lynchpin in order for freedom to be gained, recalling the past does bring greater understanding of the wrong messages conveyed, and so the job of demolishing each of these lies can take place. This is where Pippa will really need our help. It is so important that she is believed and that there are stable people around her who are prepared to listen to the stories that will gradually emerge within her healing sense of identity.

Warning: what you hear will not be 'nice'. In fact, some of her story may shock us to the core. So when we, as a church or Christian community, are considering how best to support someone like Pippa, it will be important to spend time and prayer finding those who are able to handle the extreme and heart-rending accounts of childhood horrors she may recount. The receptor of such stories will certainly need a firm and solid support base of praying people.

Some of it may not be believable. But be assured, atrocity is alive and well and not only living right across the globe, but here in Britain. Where people's hearts are blackened by the deceitfulness of the enemy's schemes there is almost no barrier to the depths of depravity Satan will plumb.

Telling the story

One of the survivor's major obstacles in recounting and coming to terms with bad memories is accepting that the child who was so badly treated was indeed 'me'. 'I was there: the pathetic scrap of humanity that I see in my mind's eye in the night, or when I am talking about the past, or who creeps up on me unawares, is me. No, I really don't want to believe it.' Pippa may even come to despise that child; perhaps in her mind she is an unwashed and unwanted brat who whines or screams. She may not like her or want anything to do with this 'alien' child—but she cannot ever escape her. The only way through to real wholeness is to accept her and love her, just as Jesus does. We can help her in this by continually and consistently reassuring her that all of her is loved and accepted, whatever she may have been coerced into doing, whatever may have been done to her, however abhorrent is seems to her now. She is not condemned; not by us and certainly not by God.

The reality was that the abused child had no safe person to speak to about her personal horrors. 'We used to look at a teacher in school and think, "Wow, she's so clean, and if we tell her, she will see how dirty we are. Dirty, dirty. Dirty"' (transcript 961 of the *Oprah Winfrey Show*, 21 May 1990).

It became a huge, black, hidden nightmare that must never see the light.

Another obstacle that a person with DID has to face is overcoming the ingrained fear that she will always be punished severely if she ever told anyone else what had happened. It will have been the 'little secret' which may have become a dark and heavy burden, turning to shame that grows ever bigger as the years go by. That fear expands like a cancer, so when the first 'secret' is told, the whole system will be poised, waiting for the disaster to strike. But this is simply another dirty, rotten lie to be dismissed as such. As well as having to battle with memories, Pippa may have to grapple with immense foreboding whenever her memories are shared.

One survivor with DID, Rosie, who we met earlier, was afraid that if she told anyone about the abuse her abusers would somehow know and that she would be shot and buried, just like her aborted baby. This lady was also afraid lest abusers whom she loved would go to prison and that further harm would somehow come to other children and her siblings. As an adult she did go to the police, but she was terrified that she would be murdered or that the abusers would kidnap and torture her children.

> I would look out for cars that may run me over. I expected someone to shoot me or get me in the middle of the night. The fear and paranoia were so intense, so terrifying. The badness, the guilt I felt for telling were overwhelming and I had to fight the desire to kill myself. My head was programmed never to tell . . . The overwhelming feeling was that no one would believe me and everyone would think I had told lies and was bad . . . I thought that I would be locked up as mentally ill and drugged like Sleeping Beauty . . . Once I told the police I was sure that men in white coats would come and lock me up.

Another survivor who contacted me was told that her parents would be killed if she told of her abuse.

A swarm of angry bees

I remember one of the early experiences of telling my story in public. It was during a Freedom in Christ conference and I had been part of the teaching team, confidently talking about the place of counselling in the church. The event took place at St Andrews Church, Chorleywood, London and the atmosphere was one of faith and expectation—an easy place in which to share a personal story. I stood up full of excitement that I had such a good testimony to tell, glad of the opportunity to discharge the burden of knowing something good you think others need to know. After I had said my bit I walked down off the stage and immediately was—I can only say 'struck down'—by the most menacing apprehension, dark with fear. It felt as though I had done something very, very wrong and must take the consequences. I remember the sensation as something like a swarm of angry bees entering my mind and overwhelming me in a thick, black, stinging mass of guilt. It sprung upon me unawares and I felt disoriented and shaky. I sat slowly down next to Mike, one of the FIC team. He sensed something was wrong and gave me a hug.

There was no time to feel sorry for myself because the session had come to an end. It was coffee time; people were waiting to speak to me and were gathering around. I was hurriedly ushered into a side room. I listened to a man just out of prison, broken and distraught because he was a perpetrator of abuse and my story had struck a very uncomfortable chord for him. It was amazing what God was doing in this humble man and I was awed at God's grace, but still the 'bees' of condemnation kept buzzing in my head. It was some time later that I was able to release my own pent-up anxiety. How 'stupid' I had been at believing I could stand and tell my story. Now I am in for it. What will happen to me now; what will happen to my children, my husband?

The FIC team set me right, reminding me of what is true—not only is there no condemnation in Jesus, but I am now safe and the evil one cannot harm me. It was absolutely right that I told others of God's deliverance from the grip of the evil one. I am now released into the kingdom of light and freedom. All that good-sense talk did not quiet the bees entirely, however. I just had to sit it out and battle through in my mind the conflict between truth and lies. What will I ultimately choose to believe?

For most, discovering that telling their story does not put them in any danger, but instead brings a sense of relief, is a great revelation and provides a boost in confidence. They find that releasing their emotions and memories doesn't lead to something bad but contributes to their health and a sense of being complete. Of course, that will only be the case if they are first provided with real, unshakable hope and support. That is why it is so crucial to provide that safe environment in which to find the courage and space to disclose otherwise hidden secrets.

Emerging memories

One survivor wrote: 'I so want to be true to God and so often I wonder if I am making it all up. Acting out something. Since I am present (and yet not present) watching as from a far, far, far away place . . . aware what is happening and that I am saying those things so it must be me, and yet everything in me is crying out too—"IT'S NOT ME!!!!".'

It may sometimes feel to Pippa as though the emerging memories are simply grotesque imaginings, made up stories that are 'sick'. She may feel that she has somehow invented tales of horror and abuse and so sees herself as evil. But why would she make up that kind of thing? What can possibly be gained from giving false accounts of such foul and sordid events, especially if nobody believes them anyway?

We have learnt in recent years that memory of trauma is stored in a separate part of the brain to that of ordinary memory. So it stands to reason that recalling those memories will not feel like the same dynamic as recalling, say, what we had for dinner yesterday or where we went on holiday last summer. I listened to a survivor a few days ago who was absolutely horrified at what her alters were saying and doing. She couldn't understand where the other part of her would have got those ideas—'I have never seen a horror movie in my life, never read a thriller, where did those disgusting stories come from?' It was highly probable that she was not making it all up but that she actually lived through that experience as a child.

I can certainly testify to the sense of self-abhorrence at recounting details of sexual abuse that was bizarre and unbelievable. Where on earth did I get that kind of picture from? Brought up in a decent, hard-working family, I had never (and haven't to this day) watched a horror film, or anything even vaguely indecent. How could such a vision enter my head? I must either be evil or sick in the mind. I clearly remember shouting at Christopher that I am making it all up, he mustn't listen to me. I am bad. It is all lies. It was a most painful and heart-wrenching period, as I had to face the possibility that it was, indeed, all true.

By remembering and speaking it out Pippa is able to 'hear her own story' and in so doing she gains an understanding of where the truth lay (that these things actually happened to her) and where lies (that I am bad or dirty) came from. She can go on to grasp the fact that she is now safe in the arms of Jesus and in the, albeit quite fallible, shelter of his Body. How wonderful for her to come to realise that nothing that has happened to her, or indeed may ever happen to her, can change who she is in Christ. Bad things may have taken place in her life; she may have been coerced into doing evil, horrible things. But whatever has occurred in the past, she is now a beloved child of God who is clean and pure in Him. There is absolutely no cause for shame or disgrace. She is found 'in Christ' and as such, is totally and unconditionally accepted as pure and clean; there is now no condemnation for her. ('Therefore there is now no condemnation for those who are in Christ Jesus' Romans 8:1.) She will never, ever be separated from him. ('For I am convinced that neither death nor life, neither angels nor demons . . . nor anything else in all creation, will be able to separate us from the love of God that is in Christ Jesus our Lord' Romans 8:38, 39.) Nor will he ever forsake or abandon her. ('Do not be afraid or terrified . . . for the Lord your God goes with you; he will never leave you nor forsake you' Deuteronomy 31: 6, Hebrews 13:5.)

The alters and memory

Alters do, of course, hold all the sordid details of the inside story. As the recovery journey progresses, changes will be taking place constantly within the system of alters. You can expect a gradual unfolding, as Pippa and her alters corporately become more secure in their sense of who they/she is in Christ. The safer Pippa feels, the more likely it is that we as helpers and supporters will meet alters. That may mean that angry, frightened or aggressive parts appear. It may seem that the more she receives help and support, the worse things get. We mustn't be deceived into feeling discouraged. It may be necessary for some of these alters to make an appearance and learn firsthand that whatever they say and do they will not be condemned or punished. While bad or inappropriate behaviour must not be tolerated, it will be a really good lesson for them (the alters) to learn that they are loved unconditionally. So while boundaries must be put in place, Pippa will also be learning the lesson that God's grace covers them in all situations.

One morning in therapy with Christopher, an alter, whom he hadn't met before, appeared. She suddenly jumped up and became agitated, angry and out of control, pacing up and down the room, kicking the sofa and bashing the venetian blinds with her fist. *Of course* she was angry—we had been talking about horrific treatment at the hands of adults who should have been protecting me. However, damaging furniture, or ourselves, was not to be tolerated. Christopher was very clear on that. He calmly stayed seated and, while reaffirming how understandable our outrage was, he laid down the ground rules. No destruction. No abuse. Those kinds of boundaries are as important as affection—love has to be stronger than the emotions that the survivor feels or she will feel insecure and uncertain of what she can and cannot do.

Pippa's renewed mind

As the alters are wrestling with all these new messages of love and forgiveness, trying to fit them into what they have up till now believed, Pippa has a huge job to do in re-learning things about herself and the world—in other words, renewing her mind. The memories will have to be reframed in order for them to fit in with a new way of thinking. Pippa herself does the reframing in light of her changing world view. That is, exchanging all the lies in her mind for the truth as revealed in God's Word. Our job is to assist in that task by immersing her in the truth.

It makes perfect sense to present the Gospel message to each alter who is ready to talk to us. Just as a double-minded man is unstable (James 1:8), so a person will be unstable who has some parts of her personality aligned to God and other parts which are unsure or loyal to the enemy. Jesus came to bring down the dividing walls of hostility (Ephesians 2:14) and also to destroy the works of the evil one (1 John 3:8). His message is one of reconciliation (2 Corinthians 5:18). That is his will in every individual too, not least those who are fragmented. So in bringing each alter to a saving knowledge of Christ, we are helping them to be 'one' and so submit every part of themselves to him, in much the same way all of us need to submit every area of our lives and personalities to him.

However, we must be careful not to make this a pressurising factor for them. The Gospel is to be *offered* and each alter given every chance of fully understanding the good news and surrendering to it. But they must not be manipulated or coerced. They are multiple in the first place because they were forced to do things they did not want to do; they were controlled to the point that they lost all sense of self; they were cruelly lured into abusive, painful and dangerous situations and given no choices. **Those**

circumstances must not be repeated. The sufferer will have antennae that will pick up any sign of manipulation a mile away and will make no progress if that is on our agenda.

Remember these people are survivors and they will, as a corporate whole, cope with boundaries. What is vital is that we stay calm, following through all promises that we have made, reminding them constantly of the truths of who they really are and of what God has done for them and given to them. Constant reassurances of our love and of God's ability to stay with them, fight for them and fill all their needs, are usually the most powerful and stabilising things we can do. Providing a safe and reliable environment within a loving community that is able to model truth is the fertile ground in which fragile faith can grow.

Make sure there are plenty of opportunities for the alters to come and express what they need to. Every individual is different and some want and need more time for his/her alters than others. Also, Pippa's needs will change depending on the stage in her healing journey. As a general rule, find a place where she can allow the alters to speak at least once a week. Teach her how to care for and listen to the alters herself. Help her to find a safe place—her room at home, a quiet place in the park or a room in the church building, for example—where she can go if the alters need to come and draw or write or play alone.

One key to unlocking much that has been bound up for a long, long time is having definite times in the diary when Pippa can allow her alters, or herself, to express fears and to talk through current issues. A regular time for uninterrupted self-disclosure is a major tool the Lord can use to show her who she really is, what has really happened and how he can put her together again. It is amazing how a badly hurting person can manage to hang on, even when things are tough, as long as they know there is a time coming when she can talk, cry or offload in a safe place. This is where it is helpful, though not always essential, to have on hand experienced counsellors.

This structure is important both for Pippa and for those caring for her. In between the times of sharing the pain are times when she will just have to trust God for herself, alone. I experienced many times when the memories or emotions felt overwhelming. Those were the times when I had to choose to lean back on what I had learnt during easier times. Those were the times I grew in my faith and confidence in God.

At the same time, we as helpers need to have breaks when we don't have to focus on someone else's pain. These times of stepping aside allow room for her to develop her own relationship of trust in Jesus, and for us to be refreshed. All concerned in Pippa's recovery journey need to have a solid and vital relationship with God. Our understanding of the world of the Spirit really helps us all to move on in becoming like Jesus.

Chapter
11

SPIRITUALITY 1—The good, the bad and the ugly

'The reason the Son of God appeared was
to destroy the work of the enemy.'
1 John 3:8

'We are not human beings having a spiritual experience.
We are spiritual beings having a human experience.'
Pierre Teilhard de Chardin

God is able to heal all who come to him. However, the 'all' are not always in a position to receive that healing. In many cases, deeply troubling events have had a physical effect on the organ of the brain, causing behaviours that would lead to difficulty later in life, and so the healing required from God would include a physical component as well as emotional and psychological elements. That said, much of our lives are governed by the supernatural (perhaps far more than we in the West are prepared to admit to) and we must address those issues.

Christians have tended to polarise in the way they approach the spiritual origins of mental health conditions. Kierkegaard wrote: 'There are two ways to be fooled: one is to believe what isn't so; the other is not to believe what is so.' That is no more true than in recognising the activity of the forces of evil in our world. Some see demonic activity behind every negative issue and want to 'deliver' a struggling person from the demon or demons they see as responsible. Others have gone to the opposite extreme and concentrated on the psychotherapeutic angle alone, effectively ignoring the reality of the spiritual world. Genuine mental illness exists and some conditions have organic causes, some have emotional, some have spiritual, but most are a combination of all three. Therefore, all these issues, including the spiritual, must be addressed if we want to help Pippa and others with DID.

Some people are in danger of spiritualising everything and forgetting that something as mundane as everyday choices are often at the heart of the problem. Time spent with Pippa does not have to be all about prayer. Of course, prayer has its place, but it is important that we actually speak directly to Pippa and her alters. We are sometimes tempted to simply address everything to God, as if by closing our eyes and asking God to do something, Pippa's situation will miraculously get better. Occasionally that can be used by well-meaning helpers as a scapegoat. Pippa needs a meaningful relationship with us; she needs to know that we have heard her and have felt what she is feeling, at least in some part. She wants an honest encounter with us—we are 'God with flesh on' to her. We must look at her, make eye contact, give her our full attention and listen with all of our being.

If Jesus were here in the flesh he would not respond to Pippa's cry for help by holding a prayer meeting. He would give her his full attention and all-embracing love; he would speak gently to her, with instruction and encouragement—just as he did with Blind Bartimaeus (Mark 10:46-52), Nicodemus (John 3:1-21), the blind man at the Pool of Bethesda (John 5:1-15) and many others. He addressed their immediate issues and often asked something of them. He formed a significant relationship with those who came to him and often made physical contact with them. The one time he did actually pray was when his friend was already dead! When he did appeal to God his Father, he made it plain that he did so for the benefit of his hearers.

Satan's influence

If we adopt a Biblical world view, we will recognise that we are made up of body, mind and spirit and so need to address the needs of all three aspects of any individual when leading them into freedom, including, and especially, those of the spirit. In recognising the reality of the spiritual world, we are forced to see the role that Satan plays in our lives. While he is not the cause of every negative issue, spiritual causes of illness are common. If a young child is exposed to evil actions it makes sense to conclude that the source of evil will continue to have an influence in his or her life as they grow older. Unless, that is, they are surrounded by those able to counteract that influence in the name of Jesus— and also show them how to do that. Satan will continue to influence us until we make the bold step to refute and renounce him, and order him out of our lives.

When Pippa tells us about horrific things in her life done by people driven by evil forces, then we must show her how she can rid herself of such influences. There are two parts to that process. The first involves saturating herself in truth as found in Jesus—the Word of God in all its forms. The second part is renouncing any participation she has had in evil, through actions, words and thoughts: basically, repentance. This is important even if she did not choose to say or do those things but acted under pressure.

Then comes the positive part: accepting the forgiveness and cleansing that Jesus offers and completely believing it; living life in the light of who she now is: a cleansed and redeemed child of God, holy and chosen, precious and beloved. One psychiatrist in a mental hospital in Northern Ireland during the time of the 'Troubles' told me, 'If my patients really understood about Christ's forgiveness, my wards would empty tomorrow.'

It is likely that there are parts of Pippa's system with wrong conceptions or harmful allegiances and it will be tempting to bulldoze in and completely demolish all that we see as wrong. Her view of God, perhaps also of Satan or of evil, was formed when she was very tiny and is very much an integral part of who she is and of how she relates to herself and others. It would not be kind to smash that mercilessly. Be patient and honour her.

When I was working in California I received a publication written by and for multiples (people with DID). Many of the contributors wrote of their experiences of the 'Light', of being 'one with the universe', or familiar with guardians, angels and spirit guides. Yes, the 'Prince of Darkness' does disguise himself as an angel of light, and yes, there may well be demons lurking in the dark corners of the mind. But we must be so careful not to quickly condemn. In receiving teaching about the truth, she will be in a better position to sift out for herself what is of God and what is not. With our help (and the Freedom in Christ 'Steps to Freedom' process is really helpful in this, see the back for details), she will accomplish that herself. But giving her the message that she has got it wrong too soon or too forcefully may demolish any fragile sense of worth that is emerging.

Crystals and clangers

One day when I was living in California, Mel was referred to me from an eminent psychiatrist in town. She was a survivor of ritual abuse and had been struggling in recovery for twelve years. She was a small, plump person, well dressed, timid, with a round, rosy, likeable face, but with a look of great sorrow in her eyes. She had been with me for only a short time when a four-year-old alter emerged who was very frightened and confused, referring all the time to a large crystal Mel wore around her neck. She seemed to think that in it was her only hope of survival, insisting that she had to 'commune' with it and the many other crystals like it that she had at home. Even though she saw herself as a Christian believer the child alter lived in fear of doing anything that would prevent her from touching those pieces of polished rock. When the adult Mel came back she was uncompromising about her need for the spiritual help and protection these gave her.

In my zeal I felt it was my duty to enlighten Mel of the complete folly in trusting in what are at best bits of old stone and, at worse, the tool of demons. Even though I spoke in gentle tones I effectively flattened the whole of her fragile belief system, threatening to destroy the tentative fabric of her hopes for survival. Without spending time winning her trust and forming a caring and stable relationship, I couldn't possibly hope to offer her real and lasting help. She, not surprisingly, rejected me and I never saw her again. I was not wrong in seeing the crystals as a threat to her recovery, even her eternal salvation, but I was wrong in failing to recognise that this dear lady was clinging onto the only hope she felt she had and I should not have tried to pull it down before first giving her something far better in its place. I hope I will not drop that clanger again.

People with DID often appear to be particularly sensitive to spiritual reality; their inner antennae seem to be tuned in to a spiritual atmosphere. When I was in the most intense stage of my recovery, a number of my child alters were claiming to have seen, indeed continued to see, both angels and demons. They were perfectly comfortable, delighted, in fact, in the presence of angelic beings and would routinely tell me and others when they were present and what they looked like. Often, they were able to explain why they were there. They were less comfortable with demons, though they were not totally afraid of them. They had learnt to accept that their presence was a part of life. When five-year-old JuJu was aware if a group of demons were in a room (they were almost always in a group), she would tell us, but was not overly frightened, just wary.

It makes perfect sense for a young child to develop a hyper-awareness of everything that was going on around her. The slightest change could signify that bad times were coming. She needed to be alert so that she could prepare herself—in many cases this meant switching to another state of consciousness, another alter personality, in order to bear an otherwise unbearable situation.

Satanic Ritual Abuse

A high proportion of people with DID are the survivors of what is known by some as Satanic Ritual Abuse (SRA). These extreme forms of abuse inflicted on vulnerable children and adults have called for extreme measures to ensure survival, hence the existence of DID for them.

Satanic Ritual Abuse is a reality here and now in the UK and across the world. What exactly is it? According to Valery Sinason, Consultant Child Psychologist and international authority on ritual abuse, it is:

> the involvement of vulnerable children and adults in sadistic acts of physical, emotional, spiritual and sexual abuse that often occur at ceremonies at specific times of the year. By linking abuse to religion, magic or the supernatural the victim is made to feel intrinsically bad. The fear is instilled that they, their families or those they love will be killed in this life and doomed in an after-life if they do not obey and stay silent. (Quoted from a briefing organised by The Committee on Ritual Abuse and Dissociation held in the House of Commons, 30 November 2011.)

Things have moved on in the last 10 or 15 years within the British police force and abuse is now taken more seriously. Unfortunately, that is not always so with Satanic Ritual Abuse. Cases of ritual abuse are hugely under-reported and their investigations underfunded. In the 1980s and early 1990s the media seized on a number of reported of satanic abuse of children: in Rochdale, Nottingham, Manchester, Durham and South Ronaldsay in the Orkney Islands. In the late eighties a government inquiry into Satanic Abuse, led by Professor Jean la Fontaine, concluded that Satanic Ritual Abuse did not exist. '"Children were influenced into making false claims by grown-ups dominated by evangelical Christian extremists. Over-anxious adults dealing with distressed children had come to the conclusion that satanic abuse must be to blame", said Prof la Fontaine' (*Daily Express*, Friday, 3 June 1994). That report discredited those who had tried to bring such practices to light, and questioned the integrity of those working with survivors. We are thankfully now in an age where the exposure of 'cover-ups' and secrecy is popular and this kind of abuse is at last becoming accepted, at least in some quarters.

> At one point we denied the very existence of any form of abuse of children. Sadly we finally had to face this. Then we denied that people with learning disabilities ever suffered abuse and we had to face that also. Until we face the existence of ritual abuse we will never be able to take steps to prevent and treat those vulnerable people who suffer. (Christiana Horrocks OBE, formerly director of Voice, quoted in TAG website (www.tag-uk.net), 2006.)

The dilemma of proof

Satanic Ritual Abuse is still incredibly difficult to prove. Police and solicitors don't know where to start and the crimes involved are difficult to prosecute. It is also hard for survivors to get legal advice. Although it is the case that there is a growing awareness of ritual abuse in Britain both in the medical profession and in government, there is still a long way to go before justice seen to be done. It is a highly charged field and some who are working to bring justice to these victims are ridiculed, and their work belittled.

One such investigator was a woman police officer with 20 years' experience. She was appointed to investigate cases of ritual abuse but was dismissed from her post before her report was authorised and has been unable to access it since. Her hard work was apparently unrecognised and the immensely important findings have still not come into public knowledge. There are a growing number of high profile cases believed to be instances of SRA and even household names and famous personalities are implicated in satanic practices involving the abuse of children. Much still needs to be done to bring the full extent of these horrendous crimes beneath the scrutiny of the British justice system.

Recent examples include the high profile cases in Peterborough, London, Llanelli and Kidwelly. There is the case of 'Adam' whose torso was found in the Thames in 2001; the case in May 2009 of seventeen-month-old Peter Connelly ('Baby P'), whose body was found with fifty injuries; and Kristy Bamu, the fifteen-year-old who was killed on Christmas day 2012 by his sister and boyfriend who accused him of being a witch. These are all reportedly due to ritual abuse. We could add many more, but each case is not really cut and dried. In the past ten years police have investigated 83 deaths reportedly to be ritual in nature, of which four were of children, the most well known being that of Victoria Climbie in 2000.

Sometimes the rituals are not obviously in the name of 'Satan'. There was a recent programme on BBC television showing the abuse of a five-year-old boy in the Congo, who was accused of being a witch. The filming was edited to exclude the worst offences, but horrified viewers still watched as this terrified little boy, surrounded by angry 'Christian' church leaders, was slapped, kicked in the stomach, given an enema and not allowed to defecate, and locked alone in the church building for three days and nights in the soaring African heat, with no food and very little water. This was all in the name of religion—in this instance, 'Christianity'. The purpose was to rid him of demonic 'possession'. That was ritual abuse. This modern-day surge in the apparent awareness and 'treatment' of demonic possession is known in some African communities as 'kindoki'. That is not unlike the kind of abuses that have historically taken place throughout the world and in every age. (For more on the street children of Kinshasa see www.fotovisura.com/child-witches-of-kinshasa. This contains some disturbing images.)

It appears that abuse of this kind can take place anywhere. While we must not go overboard, we must also make sure that we are aware of the existence of this heinous and dangerous treatment of the innocent and take every step possible to lead its victims into healing and promote every effort to prevent it from happening. This is would be no simple task. Children have been victims of abuse within their family networks for thousands of years and in every culture. That ritual abuse has been uncovered, and more specifically Satanic Ritual Abuse, is a credit to the many people who are now working towards the acceptance by professionals that this happens, and that it takes place in the twenty-first century.

This is becoming more widely accepted but even 25 years ago this was documented: 'In severe cases, even a child's physical development can be affected, with retardation of menstrual cycles and breast development in females and chest-hair growth and sexual function in males' (Kathleen Roney-Wilson, 'Healing Survivors of Satanic Sexual Abuse' in The Journal of Christian Healing Vol. 12, No. 1, Spring 1990). It is certainly true that physical as well as psychological scars remain long after the abuse ends. I myself failed to thrive as a child and my physical growth has been permanently stunted.

Many learnt through experience early on in their lives that their abusers' worship or veneration of personified evil has been at the core of their abuse. (Other abusers may play at religion as a context in which to have power over their victims.)They may have experienced appalling mistreatment and torture at the hands of those who worship Satan or who have committed these despicable things in his name. Because of this, their testimonies are unlikely to be taken seriously and are dismissed or, worse, they are accused of fabricating their stories and given some inappropriate label of mental illness.

This is just what Satanists intended. They have been drawn into the lie that they will be given power if they desecrate that which is pure, good or innocent. Therefore small children are a perfect target; their innocence is desecrated and their purity sullied by every kind of violation. By the time a survivor reaches adulthood they are usually fully convinced that their word, like everything else about them, is of no value.

It is clear that there is widespread cynicism and unbelief regarding the existence of SRA. However people who have listened to a victim remembering the past will testify to power and depth of their pain, with the experience etched deeply on their own memory. Their obvious distress would be impossible to fabricate. Part of their anguish is the confusion they face about their own guilt in the events they recall. One of the aims of satanic groups is to discredit the victim. Indeed, by destroying the child's belief in him/herself this is not difficult. When Pippa recalls the event, as the present adult or through an alter, she feels the impact of how wrong, bad, evil those actions were and is painfully aware of her part in them. The guilt and shame can be crushing.

The sort of cruelty the child would have had to endure is extreme and repulsive. Why doesn't an abused child tell a safe adult about what is happening to him/her? Pippa, as a survivor of such repugnant maltreatment, may have been too young to be able to express her experiences in words, or perhaps her parents or carers took part in the rituals. She may have been subjected to what is known as 'psychic surgery': the child would be told that a time bomb, monster or evil spirit has been planted in her body through surgery and if she tells, the bomb will go off, or the monster or evil spirit will take control of her body (I had personal experience of this).

Satanic Ritual Abuse

What does it typically entail? (Please note that some of the insistences described below may be disturbing.)

1. The use of fire to threaten and burn the child, often in places which will not be seen by others.
2. Extended, severe and bizarre types of sexual abuse.
3. Threats of death and demonstrations that the perpetrators possess magical or supernatural powers.
4. The use of knives to cut the child and remind him or her that he or she has no power in any of these situations.
5. The child being tied down or locked up for extended periods of time, usually alone; sometimes being buried.
6. Chanting in a rhythmic, singsong tone, using words to convince the child that she or he now belongs to the devil and can never be free.
7. The administration of hallucinatory drugs and/or herbal tranquilizers.
8. The smearing of the child with blood or animal faeces, or being made to ingest these things.
9. Sometimes it includes cannibalism, child sacrifice and other promiscuous and torturous abuses.

In these cases mind programming is often a major problem to be faced and dealt with in the recovery journey. Fear and anxiety are the dominant issues here for Pippa today, as in the original abuse—what will they do to me next? What will they make me do to others?

Children abused in SRA are often put in a double bind: 'You kill that other child or we will kill the child, and you'; 'You torture him (hurt him, torment him) quickly or we will torture him slowly.' In your eagerness to hear Pippa's full story, don't press for disclosure until she is ready. There is a very complex tangle of beliefs and automatic reactions which connect her understanding to your kindness and what you say may not be what she hears. This may be the time to seek out the support and advice of people who have training and experience in handling traumatic memories. However, if you are able to stay with the survivor, see it through, without panicking or showing any signs of repulsion of him/her, you are communicating something very powerful—the God you know and follow is not shocked or overwhelmed by these disclosures, that you totally believe that he can bring her to a place of wholeness, and as his people you and the Truth Team or support network will be by their side.

Occasionally I had rung a support person to tell them about another flashback or newly emerged memory, only to have the response 'so what?'. Sounds harsh, but it was a good question. So what if I now know that something else abusive had happened to me. Does that change who I am now? No. Does that make me a different person? Does that mean I am bad or dirty? No. In fact, all it does is make me more aware that my God has delivered me out of the hands of evil people, and restored me and made me clean and free.

Chapter
12

SPIRITUALITY 2—Aware and alert

'Be self-controlled and alert. Your enemy the devil prowls
around like a roaring lion looking for someone to devour.
Resist him firm in your faith, because you know
that your brothers throughout the world are
undergoing the same kind of sufferings.'
1 Peter 5:8, 9

'Nothing is a waste of time if you use the experience wisely.'
Auguste Rodin

Almost every DID person I have ever met seems to have had a heightened spiritual awareness. Many are in touch with a reality that is not restricted to the physical/material realm. It is true that for all of us, our minds are able to reach beyond the concrete reality of computers, shops and pizzas. In fact, there may be times when that non-material world is even more real for the survivor than what we can see and hear. As well as people, a multiple's inner world may indeed contain trees and hills, rooms and cushions, but not in the way we know them. There may be some concept of space, though probably not of time; there may even be more than one dimension.

I once counselled a lady who had one realm on the inside for her children and another for the adults. They lived on separate plains and were forbidden to mix except with the very rare permission of an inside entity who took the shape of a great bird who reigned supreme over all matters to do with her alters. This bird-like part forbade the adults to talk to the children and stopped any of the alters speaking to me, the counsellor, unless he felt it was safe to do so. The purpose of the great bird's absolute rule was to preserve the safety and secrecy of the inside system. Every system is carefully worked out in a way which is thought to preserve sanity and keep secrets.

Unhelpful assumptions

It is not uncommon for a person with DID to act in an uncharacteristic way or to speak with a strange voice. They may behave like a small child or be overly aggressive, even violent. Although we now understand that alters are making an appearance at such times, many are still ignorant of that fact. Christians in some branches of the church will interpret such behaviour as demonic and assume that deliverance prayer is the answer. The trouble is, however many prayers are prayed and commands are made, the alter will not, indeed cannot, be cast out.

However, it could also be true that an alter is demonised or that a personality that appears to be an alter turns out to be a demon masquerading as an alter. If there has been occult involvement in the past—and of course many with DID are survivors of SRA (see the previous chapter)—there will almost certainly be some significant demonic issues that needs to be dealt with.

This need not faze us. With some sensitive questioning and listening to the Holy Spirit, we can discern whether we are dealing with an alter, a demon, or an alter who is demonised. It will gradually become obvious. We must stay in that place of learning from God as we takes steps together to understand our DID friend. Jesus always 'turns up' and we will be amazed at the way he really does turn all things together for our good (Romans 8:28).

Prayer and deliverance

We have been taught to pray for the sick and suffering. Indeed, we are instructed to call for the elders when we are sick that they may pray for us (James 5:14). There are, however, surprisingly few references to clear instructions about praying for sick people, even though there is no doubt at all from scripture that God does and will heal. So we must be circumspect in the way we think about how God may want to heal. Many times we find Jesus asking the sick, anxious or suffering person to respond to him in some way, to obey his instructions. So we cannot simply expect healing for ourselves or others without some engagement between the will of the one who needs prayer and God himself.

In many church environments, a typical scenario is for a survivor like Pippa to be placed in the middle of a group of people for prayer. She may be seated while the pray-ers are standing around her. In this case somebody would be standing behind her, outside her field of vision. She may then be asked questions, perhaps touched, or incomprehensible words may be spoken over her as others pray in tongues.

I well remember these times of prayer in the early days of recovery. They were so reminiscent of my original abuse it was hard to remain cool and unafraid. Not that I understood why I felt so uncomfortable in those times; I was not yet aware of the alters, nor even of the abuse. My mouth would be dry, particularly if this was a planned session, and I had had hours or days to become nervous about it. My palms would be sweaty and I would feel inadequate, self-conscious and very, very small. My mind would go blank at each question and I would feel stupid and misunderstood. With pounding heart and shaking hands I would try to calm myself down enough to sound sensible.

Questions over, the group surrounding me would stand and I would remain seated—or even if I stood everyone else was so much taller than me that I felt overwhelmed with their power and my helplessness. Hands would be placed on my body—my head, or my back or my heart, sometimes on other parts of me. That would be the last straw and even as I held on to my thin and fragile self-control, the room would fade into the distance and I would dissociate into someone else.

I was sometimes aware of screaming or swearing, of kicking or struggling. I believe at times I would attempt to run out of the door and heavy hands and rough arms would keep me in. Even as I write this, the awful confusion, the despair and the utter terror that engulfed me at those times is returning to me. It is not a pleasant sensation.

Though kind, these people didn't understand. They simply weren't aware that they were recreating, in part, a similar scenario that caused my terrified self to divide in the first place. What was happening was not, as they thought, a demon coming and arguing with them, but a part of myself trying hard in the only way it knew to protect me from further trauma. *Of course* there would be struggle and aggression—it was as if the abuse was about to happen all over again. My alters did not understand that this was not the 1960s. I was no longer a defenceless child but an adult with choices to make and strength to carry them out.

These experiences gave me a sense of dark and dreadful abandonment that was only a little less terrifying than the original trauma. Based upon my own experience, prayer has the potential to be fraught with hazards for the survivor. If, in addition to prayer for healing, the ritual of deliverance is also added, things would get worse. My extreme, perhaps noisy and disturbing responses would alert the people praying to the possibility that it was not me but a demon or demons causing the violent reaction. The prayers would become louder, more urgent, more authoritative and altogether more frightening. The aggression would seem to be directed at me or something in me and even though my adult mind understood what was going on, my alters did not. It was as if I was at the receiving end of anger and that could only mean one thing—I had done something wrong and would be punished.

It may well be that there is a case of demon oppression or 'demonisation' (it won't be demon 'possession' if they are born-again Christians), but it is not deliverance prayer that is necessary. Rather, we need to help Pippa to identify the issues in her life that have 'opened a door' for the enemy to gain a foothold. Sometimes this is merely that they have been abused, but there may still be some attitude or wrong action that hasn't been dealt with that has enabled the enemy's influences to enter her life. Bear in mind that fear is still something that God says we don't need to have: 'perfect love drives out fear, because fear has to do with punishment. The one who fears is not perfected in love' (1 John 4:18). If we are completely in tune with God, fear will have no place in our lives. Pippa's dreadful early trauma has caused fear and other ways of coping with life that are outside of God's perfect way for us to be deeply established in her mind and heart. We have to give her the opportunity to turn her back on these unhelpful actions and attitudes; to 'repent' to use a Biblical word, to renounce them, turn right around and face the right way, that is, to look at Jesus.

Without resolving those things and introducing godly attitudes to replace wrong ones, the enemy will continue to have a place in her life. Pain, through bitterness, resentment, unforgiveness and anger, will cause a great deal of emotional and physical problems. These may also prevent alters from integrating because it will simply not feel safe to do so. The world will still feel a dangerous and unstable place. In that case, no amount of wisdom and good advice will enable Pippa to find her freedom. The best we could do is help her to cope with her life issues, but this would be to short-change her.

The Corinthian Christians were giving ground to the enemy through jealousy and quarrelling and Paul explained they were therefore unable to receive the 'solid food' of deeper teaching:

> I gave you milk, not solid food, for you were not yet ready for it. Indeed, you are still not ready. You are still worldly. For since there is jealousy and quarrelling among you, are you not worldly? . . . Do not deceive yourselves. If any one of you thinks he is wise by the standards of this age, he should become a 'fool' so that he may become wise . . . all

things are yours . . . and you are of Christ, and Christ is of
God. (1 Corinthians 3:2, 3, 18, 21, 23)

It is highly likely that many of these Corinthian Christians
had also experienced trauma. Whatever the reasons for their
conflicts, they still had to resolve their sin issues before they
could understand and enjoy the deeper things of God which
leads to spiritual maturity.

So with us, we must all, including Pippa, deal with
unresolved sin as far as we are able, before we can move on.
When these issues are dealt with, the enemy will no longer
have any grounds to stay and will simply be compelled to
leave: 'Submit yourselves, then, to God. Resist the devil, and
he will flee from you' (James 4:7). There is no mention here
of any loud or aggressive deliverance prayer. In fact, all the
work is done between the survivor and the Lord.

Pippa's power

Like the rest of us, Pippa will have to do this for herself,
although we can support and guide her. She has the
responsibility and the authority to renounce the wrongdoing
in her life, repent and turn away from it and announce
that she is fully submitted to the will of God for her. This is
not about casting out demons. It is about each individual
submitting to God and resisting the devil. As Pippa, with
Molly, Jimmy and any other alters, expose themselves to the
truth as it is found in Jesus, strongholds of the enemy can be
dealt with. When no footholds remain she can tell the enemy
to leave; to go; to 'shove off'. Demons have no choice at this
point but to 'flee' (James 4:7).

It is a great revelation to most people that they have the
power in Christ to take that authoritative stand themselves
and don't have to wait for a 'qualified' or more 'anointed'
person to come and do it for them. It is an invaluable
lesson to learn. With some encouragement, Pippa will soon
become adept at using the power inherent in her as a child
of God to submit to God and boldly resist the devil and his
lies. Freedom comes as each alter, as necessary, decides

to turn away from the lies and footholds of the enemy and embraces who they are in Christ. Pippa is no different from the rest of us; the key to living a free life in Christ is to be constantly aware of times when we are allowing sin to jeopardise the peace of Christ in our lives. (There is a helpful appendix by Steve Goss in my book, *Am I a Good Girl Yet?*, that outlines how dealing with a demonic issue was key in my own journey to freedom.)

The reality is, of course, that all of us—not just those with DID—need to deal with the mental rubbish in our lives in order to remove the enemy's hold and move on.

As already mentioned, you may find that some alters, because of direct involvement with the occult or due to the evil nature of their abuse, have become demonised (that is, oppressed or strongly influenced in some way by a demonic spirit). That is possible even if the core personality does not appear to be directly influenced by the demonic. In that case we deal with it in exactly the same way as we would if it were Pippa. If alters have enough decision-making ability to choose the wrong way, then they will have what it takes to choose the right way.

The support we give someone like Pippa who has been trapped in the clutches of the enemy will stir Satan's anger: 'Your enemy the devil prowls around like a roaring lion looking for someone to devour' (1 Peter 5:8). Note: he cannot touch us unless you give him permission.

Satan—the great clatterer
St Frances de Sales (1567-1622) has an interesting take on this:

> Our enemy is a great clatterer, do not trouble yourself at all about him. He cannot hurt you. Mock at him and let him go on. Do not strive with him; ridicule him, for it is all nothing. He has howled round about all the saints, and made plenty of hubbub, but to what purpose? In spite of it all, there they are, seated in the place which he has already lost—the wretch! (*Spiritual Conferences, Book 111. Letter to Mme de Chantal, a widow*)

We must teach Pippa—and remind ourselves—that we are completely safe seated as we are with Christ in the highest of places: 'God raised us up with Christ and seated us with him in the heavenly realms in Christ Jesus' (Ephesians 2:6). The enemy **cannot** harm us, but vigilance is imperative—keep your spiritual armour on (see Ephesians 6:10-18). As helpers we, too, must be alert. My experience is that those who are working with someone who has been ritually abused often find themselves going through particularly trying times; they are vulnerable. It is important to be aware of our weaknesses and our need for complete honesty with God and our need of repentance and cleansing. We rely totally on God's power to equip us; we stand firm in the faith and find prayerful people to support us.

Pippa's problems may still feel overwhelming at times. We may be tempted to think that we can't support her any more, that there must be people out there much better equipped than we are. That is a myth. Pippa may benefit from the help of her GP, psychiatric services or any other support she is offered. But in terms of the spiritual issues, she *can* overcome the enemy's schemes in her life with your encouragement and with the spiritual armour of which Paul speaks in Ephesians 6. Furthermore, we can lead her to a place of freedom. Satan can frighten and disturb us only if we let him. We are overcomers in Christ: 'For everyone born of God overcomes the world. This is the victory that has overcome the world, even our faith' (1 John 5:4).

These truths can be adapted and applied to alters too. They may, but not always, need to accept the Lordship of Jesus in their life and make the decision to trust him for their salvation. This does not mean that unless every one of Pippa's alters accepts Jesus as their Saviour then she is not saved. We all sometimes discover that parts of our life have not been totally given over to him. That doesn't mean we are not Christians, just that there is still work to be done in submitting ourselves to Jesus. The truth is that 'if you confess with your mouth that "Jesus is Lord" and believe in your heart that God raised him from the dead, you will be saved' (Romans 10:9). The alter, and/or the core personality, has to make the firm decision to give his/her mind and body to the Lord and then renounce all connections and actions where they have colluded with the enemy. They are to resist the enemy in every way and in every part (aloud and with witnesses) and then know that in so doing they, as a pure and Spirit-filled child of God, have power over the devil and his demons which have no choice but to go (see John 1:12; 1 Peter 5:6-9). 'For he has rescued us from the dominion of darkness and brought us into the kingdom of the Son he loves' (Colossians 1:13).

So Pippa's alters may need to be led to Christ and the same principles need to be applied—they will have to renounce the lies in their thinking and choose to believe and announce the truth. But once the majority, or the main ones if there are many alters, have come to Christ, the whole direction of her life will have changed and integration will naturally take place.

It is, therefore, not usually necessary for us as supporters to command the demons to leave (which is what happens in deliverance prayer). Pippa's resistance is enough. It is Jesus Christ who has conquered the powers of darkness, not us. We just speak in his name. In giving Pippa herself space to make these decisions and actions in faith, you are strengthening her faith and allowing her the privilege of discovering that she has as much authority in Christ as you. What a boost to her confidence that understanding could be.

It would also help her to have some discipleship training—the Freedom in Christ courses are excellent for this. Leading her to faith-enhancing Bible passages, helpful books or videos will all help to cement that conviction that she is free in Christ and only in him. It has very little to do with us.

Nothing is impossible with God
God is in the business of building his kingdom here on earth. He chooses us to inaugurate that kingdom; together we are the Bride who is being prepared for his Bridegroom.

He loves us; he longs to see us walking in the healing that is already ours, to see us free from the bondages in which sin has entrapped us. So even while we are doing our best to understand the way dissociation works and how we can help, we must never forget that our God is infinitely powerful. We may look at Pippa at times and wonder: how on earth we can help her through this? Well—'With man this is impossible, but with God all things are possible' (Matthew 19:26).

We are not dealing with some man-made god, who is here today and gone tomorrow. No, 'From ancient days I am he. No one can deliver out of my hand. When I act, who can reverse it?' (Isaiah 43:13). We are ministering to Pippa, loving her and leading her in the name of Jesus Christ who stills the storm, heals the sick and raises the dead. Is it not, therefore, possible for him to touch her mind and heal the wounds of the past? Of course it is. He gently leads us into green pastures as our Good Shepherd (Psalm 23, John 10), but he is also a consuming fire (Hebrews 12:29). We cannot know just how he will choose to bring healing and restoration to Pippa. It may be as she gradually opens up to his Spirit, but it is also possible for him to work miracles in a single moment.

Let us not pin God down, but be wide open for him to use us in any way that he wills. He chooses 'the foolish things of the world to shame the wise' and 'the weak things of the world to shame the strong' (1 Corinthians 1:27). Perhaps it will be through the very weakest and most vulnerable—those who have been so devastatingly abused and used that they have fragmented just to stay alive—that God will release his power to heal and deliver and spread abroad his infinite love into the darkest places of our broken world.

Chapter
13

INTEGRATION—Connecting the fragments

'I have given them the glory that you gave me, that they
may be one as we are one: I in them and you in me.'
John 17:22

'The reason why the world lacks unity and lies broken
and in heaps, is because man is disunited with himself.'
Ralph Waldo Emerson

For many Christians (though not for all), the ultimate goal
is for all the alters to integrate with the core personality.
However, the choice is with the survivor. God never
intended for us to be divided people, but 'complete in him'
(Colossians 2:10). We can offer Pippa the facts about what
God has done for her in Christ—who she really is, what he
intended her to be—and then allow Pippa herself to decide
her ultimate goal. My experience is that given that any
alter's job is to seek out the best for the whole, integration
becomes the norm. But this will not happen until each alter
is quite certain that they are in a safe and secure place in
every way.

The idea of integration can be introduced right at the
beginning of Pippa's healing journey even though it may
not actually take place until much later. The thought may
horrify her at first and that is entirely to be expected. We

must therefore put no pressure on her other than seeing it as an option.

Once the foundations upon which to build the truth blocks are in place we can then look at the way in which Pippa's dissociative functions could gradually be replaced by better ways of living. Dissociation is only a coping mechanism. It serves its purpose well all the while Pippa is in danger, but once she becomes an adult she often has more control over her life. (Unfortunately, that is not always the case. There are situations where adults are still controlled and manipulated against their will.) But, like all coping mechanisms, their value is limited. To live the way God intends is to do away with those ways of 'coping' in preference to a far better way. 'Life in all its fullness', Jesus called that new life (John 10:10). Peter spoke of an 'inexpressible and glorious joy' or as the Authorised Version of the Bible says, 'Joy unspeakable and full of glory' (1 Peter 1:8). However, for most of us, particularly those who have been abused, that kind of delirious delight and jubilation feels no more than an unattainable pipe dream.

In realising that integration will mean that all responsibility for her actions and words would then fall to her—in which case she can't point to an alter's needs as a reason or excuse—Pippa may feel quite daunted. For most, integration is not popular.

This is what some multiples have said about it:

Consciously, most multiples want to be integrated, but subconsciously, they are terrified.
Carole

Please understand that I am as afraid of who she will be as you are. As hard as multiplicity can be to live with, choosing to work towards integration is a painful and frightening process.
Susan

> To blithely speak of merging is frightening. Who will tell me right from wrong? Will I remember how to drive? Play music? What will remain and what do I do to curb the loneliness?
>
> Tony

One person with DID described integration as being like the reweaving of a torn fabric—the frayed parts are being woven back into the garment, making it whole. It is likened by one psychologist to both a birth and a death, or like a wedding, the end of one phase and the beginning of another.

One way of seeing integration is that it is like mixing two different coloured pots of paint together. If a blue pot was mixed with a red pot, not only would you get purple paint, but you would end up with twice as much as you had from just one pot. You are not losing the individual colours, but simply seeing them in a different, more integrated way, combined to create something else. If one alter merged with another, not only would their characteristics be joined and available, but there would be twice as much volume or strength—more 'you'.

Many questions will be asked and much discussion will need to take place. Gradually the idea of being whole, of sharing life that has up till then been parcelled out into lots, will become more appealing, more understandable, more logical, more God-planned.

How does Pippa travel from pain and fragmentation to the joy and oneness of which Jesus spoke? Paul spoke of renewal, in relation to our minds. In terms of freedom and joy there is clearly far more that God intends for us than any of us have yet experienced. He fully equips every believer with the capacity to experience all that he promised, whatever the past held. We already have 'every spiritual blessing in Christ' (Ephesians 1:3). Pippa has so many amazing new things to learn.

Integration is one very important step towards that 'holiday by the sea' that C. S. Lewis referred to in chapter 3. It is part of that acceptance of God's plan for us to be whole.

Learning to 'live loved'

The concept and reality of love is how we began this book. It is woven like a thread throughout and it is how we end the story. Love is something to which we can begin to open Pippa's eyes. As we, falteringly but in the way unique to each of us, enclose her into our circle of friendship, affection and acceptance, she will begin to understand the richness of God's love.

In that wonderful and disturbing story from William Paul Young's *The Shack*, Mack and Jesus are having a conversation. They are walking around a lake toward the tumbledown building in which Mack's small daughter, Missy, was killed. Mack wanted to know how he could live without the darkness of his fears:

> 'Remember, you can't do it alone. Some folks try with all kinds of coping mechanisms and mental games. But the monsters are still there, just waiting for the chance to come out.' 'So, what do I do now?' Jesus replies, 'What you're already doing, learning to live loved. It's not an easy concept for humans. You have a hard time sharing anything.' He chuckled and continues. 'So, yes, what we desire is for you to "re-turn" to us, and then we come and make our home inside you, and then we share.' (*The Shack*, Hodder and Stoughton, 2007)

That's now Pippa's goal—to learn to live loved.

For sure, only God does the healing, but his work is now accomplished in Christ (remember, 'it is finished'? John 19:30). Pippa is the one with the hard work ahead—but we must help her to see how the dynamics of dissociation has helped her to survive, yet is no longer a necessary part of her life. In fact, she may function better without that mechanism. However, moving away from dissociation in no way means losing anything at all of her personality, it just becomes more integrated: her personality traits are more *integral*, flowing together with all the other characteristics that form who she is.

Harmful emotions must continue to be dealt with, by exchanging them for positive, life-affirming ones, as Pippa works on the lies and replaces them with the truth. The memories that have been such a burden must be reframed to assure her that there is absolutely no condemnation for her in Christ. Once she is sure, there is no reason for her alters to be separate from the whole. Their job has been done. They are now free to merge with the host personality, in our case, Pippa, and enjoy a level of freedom that has been denied her for so long. One by one, or as a group or groups, they may decide to integrate. Pippa will be more relaxed and that sense of well-being that has been denied her for so long can begin to spread and pervade her body and mind.

How does it happen?

First of all, it has to be said that integration will not happen unless Pippa, and her parts, wants it to happen. This is not something we can 'do to' her. And it happens gradually, as each alter feels safe and secure and able to release whatever secrets or emotions they have kept from the host personality. Sometimes it is conscious and thought-out, at other times it has occurred without any real planning. Either way, it will not, indeed cannot, happen unless Pippa's mind is comfortable with the alter or alters merging.

The next thing to grasp is that one or more alters, if there are a number of them, may choose to integrate into another alter. In my case, 'Carolyn', an alter, seemed to be the most stable personality. I was not born Carolyn, but my core personality was too weak and broken to maintain full ultimate control, so many of the child alters chose to integrate into her. Some even integrated with JuJu who, though only five years old, was a fairly robust alter. Later, JuJu, and all she contained, integrated into Carolyn and I ultimately became who I am today. So Molly may choose to join with Jimmy or she may prefer to integrate straight into Pippa. We must respect each alter's wishes and allow them to choose their individual path to becoming whole, within the boundaries of their God-given freedom.

Integration can happen in all kinds of ways and can be different for each person, if not for each alter. It is simply a joining of two or more parts of a personality into one. I cannot tell you how to do it, or exactly what happens in the brain, because I just don't know. But I do know that each individual seems to understand how to 'do it' themselves. Sometimes it is an event, planned and prepared for. At other times Pippa's growing maturity and stability allows her alters to drop the need to keep memories and fears separate and will naturally come together as one.

Some people choose to be alone when it happens and may simply sit quietly and invite the alter(s) to become one with them. They may like to stand on a favourite stretch of beach or sit beside a lighted candle. It may happen in an unplanned moment or a long-awaited event. Others would rather make it a joyful celebration and want to share the experience with those whom they trust. Some like to sit in a circle joining hands with their friends and, out loud, invite the alter or alters to join them, thanking them for their wonderful help in keeping them alive and sane. For others, it happens in an attitude of prayer or praise, during the moment of baptism or while hugging a safe person. The choices are as wide as the imagination of the person concerned and it is almost always a very positive experience.

My own experiences of integration are many and varied. I used quite a hotchpotch of methods to invite my alters to come and join the core person, that is, the 'me' of this body I inhabited. Arguably, the most memorable is the instance of J.C. who insisted on integrating while I was under water! She always was a bit whacky, so it was no real surprise when she announced to Christopher my therapist that she wanted to be baptised, by full immersion, in front of our friends. And she wanted to integrate while in transit between death and life as it were—at the moment of immersion. That meant me having another baptism, in actual fact, other baptisms, plural.

I had already been both christened as a baby, then undergone full immersion baptism when I had chosen Christ to be my Saviour as a teenager. Yet another baptism seemed rather to over-egg the pudding. But eventually, after thinking through possible theological aberrations, I agreed. We have it all on video tape: J.C. standing in the pastor's swimming pool, surrounded by friends and friends of friends, all cheering her on. She stood in the water next to Pastor Pete and boldly announced that she had now chosen to follow Jesus for the rest of her life. Down she went into the water and up she came to the sound of singing (the people around us, not angels). But no J.C. appeared as Pastor Pete pulled me up. In fact, there was 'no one at home'. I appeared to be asleep, or unconscious. After a little persuasion from Pete, someone did come back into the body—it may have been JuJu (I can't actually remember). J.C. really had joined with me and hasn't been 'seen' since, though of course she has actually influenced my life every day since then. I remember that my drive home from the pool that day was as fast and furious—and fun—as I ever had driven before. Yes, J.C. was definitely still alive in some form in me.

Another integration I remember well was when a whole crowd of child alters made the decision that they felt strong enough and secure enough to let me have their memories and experiences and join with me. I was alone in my little flat in California, and sat on the sofa, talking to them all (how strange it is to have a conversation with yourself, out loud and know that you really are not going barmy). But I spoke gently to them. By then I understood that they needed to know that I, the one mostly in charge of the body, really did believe them and appreciate them for the part they had played in my survival. Then I invited them all, about 16 of them, to come into my mind and inhabit me in a full and complete way. (They were all *me* to start with, but were simply acting in a separate way to that of the core of my being.) That particular time felt quite emotional. I was not deeply upset, but moved that so many young, fragile and completely innocent parts would choose to come to me. That displayed such trust on their part—I suppose I was choosing to trust myself. This was no small thing. While after

J.C.'s integration there was much laughing and joking with friends and church members in the sunshine of a Californian October afternoon, this instance left me with tears rolling silently down my face, alone in the quiet of a tiny flat in a leafy Fresno suburb.

Every person is unique and will choose their method of integration in their own way. Some alters may also simply vanish; dissolve into the host personality as their sense of internal trust and safety increases. There are no rules, except to know that no alternative part leaves the survivor. They do not disappear—they cannot. The parts are integral to the host person and as such are to be welcomed and given every opportunity to understand their worth, to express what needs to be expressed and then be encouraged to become one with the total person.

Post-integration

The feelings which come after integration are not always easy to cope with, at least not at first. There is often a sense of loss, or of being unsure of how to live in this new way:

> I went from being DID straight into having to be an adult. Most people grow into being an adult and can make mistakes along the way. That didn't happen for me and therefore having to be this adult was daunting and overwhelming. There were things I should have known how to do, or how to be, and there was just a blank space in front of me because I hadn't had the chance to learn whatever it is you learn as a teenager and young adult. So everything became totally overwhelming.
> Wendy

> I would like friends and family members to know that the joining of the alters can be like the death of a beloved family member. Although joining is a sign of healing, I still grieve for the loss of a friend who was always there for me.
> Gloria

However, the only real loss is the complex way of dealing with life, for in reality nothing whatever has actually gone. All the components of the alter is still there, their memories, preferences, traits and characteristics will still all be retained even as they are now part of the whole. The core personality may take a few hours or days to learn to embrace the new elements of their more complete self, but she will soon adjust and feel more whole because of them.

Once integration of all the alters has taken place the work has not ended, rather, it has only just begun. Pippa will continue to need just as much support, encouragement and teaching as before, the only difference being that now she is a whole personality and there is no longer the complication of who to speak to and when. Pippa may still have to do battle with the lies that are deeply embedded in her mind. She may still need to be reassured many times that she is now safe in God's care, secure, accepted and significant. She will also need to learn how to handle the emotions which she has been able, up till then, to siphon off to various other parts so avoiding all the pain and discomfort they bring.

It is most important, even in the light of the joy of integration, that Pippa's Truth Team or other support network does not disband. Everything is not 'alright now'. The memories will not have magically disappeared, neither will the reality of the horrors she has experienced become any less painful to accept. In fact, the reverse may be true as she comes to terms with all that it implies. What lies ahead is the day by day walk in her new-found freedom, encompassing the challenge of keeping close to Jesus. This is when passages like John 15, where he teaches us to 'remain in the vine', to stay in a place of intimacy with him, are really pertinent: 'If you remain in me and my words remain in you, ask whatever you wish and it will be given you' (John 15:7). This is more about trust than getting what we want. The work of renewing Pippa's mind goes on in earnest as she continues to replace old lies with the liberating truth that she is utterly loved and accepted and has been all along.

A victory of grace has been won, another fragmented and hurting life has been reclaimed for the kingdom of God and there will be rejoicing both on earth and in heaven.

It is wonderful to see a person who has been so damaged and traumatised come out of the isolation in which they have lived and feel part of the community of God's people. People like Pippa can remain lonely and dysfunctional because they have not spent time in the company of emotionally healthy people. Some have pulled themselvos away from all company because of bad experiences in relationships and others have only ever known families or groups that are harmful or emotionally painful. In addition to dissociative tendencies they may have developed strong armour to resist the barbs of personal attack, but in so doing will have emotionally locked themselves in. The church can be that really safe place. We are committed to believing that what God has said in his written Word and in his Son is true. It is the truth that has and will set Pippa free.

So let's walk boldly on, arm in arm with those who are most wounded, knowing that as we move on together Jesus will be mending the fragmentation of both their shattered minds and our shattered communities. The Holy Spirit will repair, heal and rebuild as we immerse ourselves in his goodness and mercy and we will dwell in the house of the Lord forever. Then the Bride will be properly prepared for her Bridegroom, ready for that great banquet to come.

Bibliography

Anderson, Neil. T., *The Bondage Breaker*, Monarch, 2011.
—Victory Over the Darkness, Monarch, 2010.
Bounds, E.M., *Power Through Prayer*, Marshall, Morgan and Scott, 1970.
Bramhall, Carolyn, *Am I A Good Girl Yet?*, Monarch, 2005, rev. edn, AuthorHouse, 2012.
—*An Introduction to Dissociative Identity Disorder*, 2012, available from Heart for Truth.
—*Truth Teams: What, Why, Who and How?*, 2013, available from Heart for Truth.
Bennet, Ed., and G. Braun, *Treatment of Multiple Personality Disorder*, American Psychiatric Press, 1986.
Chase, Truddi, *When Rabbit Howls*, E.P. Dutton 1987
Cohen, Barry, Esther Giller and Lynn W., *Multiple Personality from the Inside Out*, Sidran Press, 1991.
Diagnostic and Statistical Manual IV (DSM IV) American Psychiatric Association, 2000
Foster, Richard, *Celebration of Discipline*, Hodder and Stoughton, 1980.
Friesen, James, *Uncovering the Mystery of MPD*, Here's Life Publishing, 1991.
—*More Than Survivors*, Here's Life Publishing, 1992.
Goss, Steve, *The Freedom in Christ Discipleship Course*, Monarch, 2004, 2010 (DVD and books available from Freedom in Christ Ministries).
Greenslade Philip, *Leadership*, CWR, 2002.
John, J., *The Return: Grace and the Prodigal*, Hodder and Stoughton, 2011.
Lewis, C.S., *'The Weight of Glory'*, Preached originally as a sermon in the Church of St Mary the Virgin, Oxford, on 8 June 1942: published in 'Theology', November, 1941.

—*The Chronicles of Narnia* Lions 1980.

Moran, Annmarie, Wrigley, Dennis and members of the Maranatha Community, *The Big Question: What On Earth Are We Doing to our Children?*, Maranatha Community, 2012.

Morgan, Alison, *The Wild Gospel*, Monarch, 2004.

Nash, Wanda, *Come Let Us Play*, Darton, Longman and Todd, 1999.

Ortberg, John, *When the Game is Over It All Goes Back in the Box*, Zondervan, 2007.

Powell, John, *Why Am I Afraid To Tell You Who I Am?*, Fontana 1975 .

Quoist, Michael, *Prayers of Life*, Logos Books, 1963.

Roney-Wilson, Kathleen, 'Healing Survivors of Satanic Ritual Abuse', *The Journal of Christian Healing,* Vol. 12 No. 1, Spring 1990.

Ross, Colin, *Multiple Personality Disorder, Diagnoses, Clinical Features and Treatment*, Wiley-Interscience Publications, 1989.

Sales, Frances de, *Spiritual Conferences, Book 111, Letter to Mme de Chantal, a widow,* www.salesianspirituality.com.

Scott, Sara, *The Politics and Experience of Ritual Abuse—Beyond Disbelief*, Open University, 2001.

Spencer, Judith, *Suffer the Child*, Pocket Books, 1989.

Stott, John, *Through the Bible Through the Year*, Candle Books, 2006.

Teicher, Martin H., 'Wounds that won't heal', *The Neurobiology of Child Abuse*, 1 Oct., 2000, see: www.danafoundation.org.

Tozer, A.W.,*The Worship-driven Life*, Monarch, 2008.

US News and World Report, 'The biology of soul murder: Fear can harm a child's brain. Is it reversible?', 11 Nov., 1996.

Vanier, Jean, *The Broken Body*, Darton, Longman and Todd, 1998.

Watson, David, *I Believe in the Church*, Hodder 1978.

Oprah Winfrey Show, Transcript of 21 May 1990.

Yancey, Philip, *What Good is God?*, Hodder and Stoughton, 2010.

—*What's So Amazing about Grace?*, Zondervan, 1997.

Young, William Paul, *The Shack*, Hodder and Stoughton, 2008.

Helpful websites

Heart for Truth—www.h4t.org.uk.
Provides training and support to any church or Christian group working with those who have been traumatised, abused or poses a pastoral challenge.

Freedom in Christ Ministry—www.ficm.org.uk
Provides excellent discipling resources for use in any church which seriously wants to be able to lead the most hurting into lasting freedom.

Positive Outcomes for Dissociative Disorders—www. pods-online.uk
Provides online information, and training seminars about DID and trauma recovery.

Trauma and Abuse Group—www.tag-uk.net
Provides education and raises awareness of dissociation, attachment, trauma and abuse recovery.

Association of Christian Counsellors—www.acc-uk.org
An organisation uniting and resourcing Christian counsellors and pastoral carers who work in a variety of areas, including trauma and abuse recovery.

Traumatic Stress education and advocacy—www.sidran.org
Provides resources to help people manage and understand trauma and dissociation.

The Pottergate Centre for trauma and dissociation—www.dissociation.co.uk
Provides information and treatment for those with dissociative disorders.

Brisbane Rape and Incest Survivor Support Centre—www.brissc.org.au/factsheets/whatisritual abuse/-fulltextversion
A thorough examination of the existence of ritual abuse.

Made in the USA
Lexington, KY
27 July 2015